The Invisible Yellow Line

Clarifying Nonprofit Board and Staff Roles

Jean Block

*Charity*Channel®
PRESS™

The Invisible Yellow Line: Clarifying Nonprofit Board and Staff Roles

One of the **In the Trenches**™ series

Published by
CharityChannel Press, an imprint of CharityChannel LLC
424 Church Street, Suite 2000
Nashville, TN 37219

charitychannel.com

ISBN Print: 978-1-938077-22-7 | ISBN eBook: 978-1-938077-35-7

Library of Congress Control Number: 2013937566

13 12 11 10 9 8 7 6 5 4 3 2

Printed in the United States of America

This and most CharityChannel Press books are available at special quantity discounts for bulk purchases for sales promotions, premiums, fundraising, or educational use. For information, contact CharityChannel LLC, 424 Church Street, Suite 2000, Nashville, TN 37219 USA. +1 949-589-5938

Publisher's Acknowledgments

This book was produced by a team dedicated to excellence; please send your feedback to editors@charitychannel.com.

We first wish to acknowledge the tens of thousands of peers who call charitychannel.com their online professional home. Your enthusiastic support for the **In the Trenches**™ series is the wind in our sails.

Members of the team who produced this book include:

Editors

Acquisitions Editor: Linda Lysakowski

Comprehensive Editor: Susan Schaefer

Copy Editor: Jill McLain

Production

In the Trenches Series Design: Deborah Perdue

Layout Editor: Jill McLain

Proofreaders: Linda Lysakowski, Jill McLain, Stephen Nill, and Susan Schaefer

Administrative

CharityChannel LLC: Stephen C. Nill, CEO

Marketing and Public Relations: John Millen

About the Author

Jean began her nonprofit career when she was thirteen years old, raising money through a backyard carnival for CARE. She was hooked. She has served as board leader, chief executive, and development director for several local, regional, and national nonprofits. She is now a nationally recognized speaker and trainer on nonprofit management, board governance, fundraising, and social enterprise through her two consulting companies, Jean Block Consulting Inc. and Social Enterprise Ventures LLC. At this printing, she has published three nonprofit books, *FUNdraising! 180+ Great Ideas to Raise More Money*, *The ABCs of Building Better Boards*, and *Fast Fundraising Facts for Fame & Fortune*, as well as several training manuals and articles. Other books are in the works. Jean is a regular speaker at national and regional conferences, and she presents live webinars through her companies and for other organizations.

Author's Acknowledgments

No one becomes successful in any profession without being open to learning from those with whom they live and work. I have had so many informal mentors (you know who you are), but at the top of the list is my husband and partner, John Block. Following closely behind are Melinda G., Jane D., John R., and many, many more. Thank you for sharing your wisdom with me.

Contents

Summary of Chapters

Chapter One: The Invisible Yellow Line. What is the Invisible Yellow Line? What does it have to do with effective nonprofit management anyway? Are we talking about football? I don't even watch football. And how do I have a conversation about football? Rest assured, this first chapter will answer these questions and prove the relevancy of the Invisible Yellow Line to effective board and staff relations.

Chapter Two: The Invisible Yellow Line in Governance. Every effective board member understands the board's essential governance role and follows the duties of care, loyalty, and honesty. But a board cannot govern effectively without information from and support of the chief executive and staff. This chapter discusses governance basics, including board duties, bylaws, policies, voting, and more.

Chapter Three: The Invisible Yellow Line in Management. Who manages the board? Who runs board meetings? Who takes minutes? Both board and staff are charged with getting the most from the time, talent, and treasure of the organization's management and volunteer resources. This chapter offers best practices in everything from meetings to minutes, evaluations to burnout.

Chapter Four: The Invisible Yellow Line in Finance. Board members must understand their fiscal and financial responsibilities if they are to govern effectively. Staff must institute the necessary internal policies and regularly report to the board so stakeholders can be assured of sound fiscal management.

Chapter Five: The Invisible Yellow Line in Planning. You've heard it before: *"Failure to plan is planning to fail."* What makes planning work? How do you keep a plan alive? Who participates in planning? What about committees? Who comes next? Read this chapter and find out.

Chapter Six: The Invisible Yellow Line in Human Resources. The Invisible Yellow Line in human resources is one of the most difficult for board and staff to define. We'll discuss key areas, including hiring, supervising and terminating, and key roles and responsibilities.

Chapter Seven: The Invisible Yellow Line in Resource Development. Whose job is it to develop the required revenue to support and sustain your mission? Who does what in resource development? Let's talk about oversight, compliance, and more.

Chapter Eight: The Invisible Yellow Line in Board Recruitment. An effective nomination process, including how to create a working nominating committee, is the topic of conversation here. The chapter includes a nominating committee matrix and outlines the process for effective board recruitment.

Chapter Nine: The Invisible Yellow Line Test. Take the test. Use this test to open lines of communication between board and staff leaders to clarify the Invisible Yellow Line in your organization.

Foreword

Long gone are the days of the "community" board—you remember those days, I'm sure. Those times when all nonprofit organizations, while passionate about their missions, were extremely casual in board and staff structure.

Times have changed, and nonprofit agencies have grown up. Nonprofit stakeholders have raised their expectations of governance, oversight, and efficient management. We expect organizations to step up and meet their fiduciary responsibilities and to manage themselves in a fiscally sound manner while focusing on mission and purpose. I have the great honor of serving as CEO of a vital nonprofit agency, complete with a vital, engaged, and educated board of directors. This was not the case in the early days, though, and while the board members cared immensely, none of us really knew how a good board should work in concert with its chief executive officer. So I went looking. If this book had been available then, it would have saved me a lot of trouble and time.

In *The Invisible Yellow Line*, Jean explains the process simply and challenges boards and staff members to be the very best they can be. She covers all the basics, from legal responsibilities to fundraising, in such a way that board and staff experiences will be memorable and gratifying. They will get it! They will realize that they will get as much from their nonprofit experience and service as they are willing to give. What an amazing discovery! Boards of directors and staff can actually be organized and productive, all while having a great time and developing a sincere sense of pride in the work of the agency.

If you invest the time to read and follow Jean's sage advice in this workbook, I guarantee that you will feel the same way.

Eileen Cook, CEO
Casa Esperanza and Casa Esperanza Foundation
Albuquerque, New Mexico

Introduction

In the forty-five plus years I've worked and volunteered in the nonprofit world as both a staff and board leader, I have often wondered if the traditional board of directors/chief executive officer arrangement is the most effective way to run a nonprofit business. Can it really work effectively? Wouldn't it be more effective to have a chief executive who runs the nonprofit and has a board of advisors with no governing authority?

Perhaps, but we would miss the opportunity to take advantage of the outside perspectives, knowledge, oversight, and expertise that a board of directors can offer our organization.

Now that I have introduced this manual with a thought-provoking question that challenges the way we've been operating for years and years, please allow me to propose that it *can* work.

I believe the key to a functioning board-staff relationship is the understanding that this arrangement is a partnership. In any functioning partnership, the partners understand their roles and support each other for successful outcomes.

For a nonprofit, making it work requires a clear understanding of the different roles that boards and staff members play in the pursuit of its mission and purpose.

Occasionally, this meshing of the different roles played by the partners managing a nonprofit can be described as a muddy mess of assumptions.

This manual is intended to be a useful tool for nonprofit leaders, both board and staff. It explores the different roles of board and staff in several key nonprofit management functions.

Chapters include a worksheet that can start a conversation of best practices that will help more clearly define the key roles of board and staff in your organization. I suggest that you ask each key player to review the assessments individually and then combine the results into one assessment to form the basis of useful conversations about how to define these roles in your organization.

I encourage you to open wide the avenues of communication while you read and work through this manual to make it a working document. Don't just read it and put on the shelf with other management books. I urge you to use it until it is used up and worn out. And then use it again. Ask questions. Challenge assumptions.

Your mission demands it!

Chapter One

The Invisible Yellow Line

IN THIS CHAPTER

···→ Defining the Invisible Yellow Line

···→ Why conversations are critical in defining roles in your organization

···→ How to use this manual

Some years ago, I was pondering the muddy mess of board and staff roles with a nonprofit I was advising. While taking a break to watch my favorite football team play, I suddenly envisioned the perfect way to describe this relationship.

The spectators who watch a football game on television or other electronic media clearly see a yellow line on the field that denotes the position of the next down. It's clear as can be. But the players on the field can't see the yellow line. It's invisible to them. It moves and at times can be hotly contested.

The working relationship of board of directors and staff in a nonprofit also has an Invisible Yellow Line.

The goal is to transition from a playing field with a muddy mess of assumptions to a partnership where all the players understand and accept their roles and your nonprofit's mission is served.

I have found that merely adopting the Yellow Line terminology often helps open an honest discussion about roles and prevents a defensive response.

It is worth noting that every organization is different. In some cases, the Yellow Line can be seen pretty clearly. At other times and in certain instances, the line *is* invisible and will continue to move as the organization deals with different issues at different times.

For example, in the early stages of a nonprofit's development, the board may have to roll up its collective sleeves and get involved in day-to-day administration. However, as the nonprofit matures, the board has to modify its role to step back away from the day-to-day and focus on its governance and fiduciary duties, allowing administrative professionals to manage the day-to-day.

The basics remain the same, however:

◆ Board = strategic direction, policy, and fiscal oversight.

◆ Staff = management and administration.

Admittedly, this is an oversimplification, because both board and staff have complementary roles to play in all areas of an effective partnership.

Case in point: A longtime friend of mine and exemplary chief executive was hired to run a fairly large nonprofit that had been without a CEO for a few months. My friend got right to work, implementing cost savings, reorganizing staffing, and getting the organization's

> Spectators who watch a football game on television or other electronic media see a yellow line on the field. It's clear as can be. But the players on the field can't see the yellow line. It's invisible to them. The same is true in the nonprofit environment. Board and staff are on different teams (even though both teams have the same goal, serving the organization's mission), and the line separating their roles is invisible, moves, and can be hotly contested at times.

programs and services on track. Within weeks, the board leader began to interfere, dropping in unannounced, meeting directly with individual staff members, tying up the experienced chief executive in meetings about internal minutia, etc.

When challenged by the chief executive to return her focus to leading the board, the board leader became hostile and renewed her efforts to interfere and manage the day-to-day.

Inevitably, the blurring of the Yellow Line became untenable and the chief executive resigned.

In this example, the roles of board and staff leader were not discussed and clarified at the beginning of the relationship. Both leaders

> Wouldn't it be great if there was just one set of rules that defined the roles of board and staff? Rules that never changed? It would surely make this nonprofit operating structure easier to understand and to work within. I've looked high and low for these rules, both as a board leader and as a staff leader, and I've never found them. The fact is, things change. Organizations evolve. People evolve. That's why I wrote this book as a manual to provide a way that board and staff leaders can *talk* about their roles and reduce the trap of assumptions and defensiveness.

food for thought

were unwilling to discuss their definition of the Invisible Yellow Line before the situation exploded. However, if they'd had an open and honest conversation *at the beginning* of the CEO's employment, many—if not all—of these issues could have been prevented.

And another thought for you to ponder. Teams have leaders. In this manual, I have defined the leader of the board as the board leader rather than the board president or board chair. Likewise, staff teams have leaders. I have called the leader of the staff team the chief executive or CEO.

Regardless of what you call yourself in your organization, consider this: teams follow their leaders. Therefore, whether you are the board leader or the staff leader, realize that you can set the example for an effective partnership or you can set up an adversarial relationship. In either case, your team will follow your lead!

So, what to do? Talk about it!

Conversations

Invisible Yellow Line issues play out under the general topic of communication. This is especially critical with regard to leaders and their roles. A lack of open and honest communication will inevitably result in suspicion and mistrust.

Dealing with issues when they are molehills before they become mountains can, and will, relieve incredible stress in the board and staff leader relationship and in the relationships of all others in your organization.

Here's another example of the importance of communication and conversations. A board leader asked me once what I thought of the practice of holding an executive session at the beginning of every board meeting. My response? "Good grief!"

Think about what this practice creates from the viewpoint of the other side of the Invisible Yellow Line: suspicion, fear, and resentment, to say the least. Executive sessions should be held rarely. Use them to discuss a serious issue regarding the chief executive's performance or a serious issue involving a member of the board, for example.

The bottom line in discussions about the Invisible Yellow Line is simply this: communicate. Openly and honestly. Clarify roles at all levels of board and staff leadership to prevent what could inevitably become stressful and unproductive relationships rife with misunderstanding and mistrust.

> The bottom line in discussions about the Invisible Yellow Line is simply this: *communicate.*
>
>
> important

How to Use this Manual

As I stressed earlier, much of the muddy mess of assumptions that can occur in defining the roles of board and staff can be cleared up with communication. That is why this manual is about "conversations" and not "fights and arguments."

Since board and staff leaders often come to the game of nonprofit management with different experiences and different expectations, this manual is designed to help even the playing field and make the Yellow Line *less invisible*.

Each chapter contains a chart with typical nonprofit team responsibilities. Use the charts to stimulate conversation about who does what. Remember that the Invisible Yellow Line is *invisible*. It will move as your organization evolves, and roles and responsibilities can shift as you strive to overcome obstacles and continue to meet and exceed the expectations of those you serve.

> Don't just put this manual on your shelf where it gathers dust and gets lost among your other management manuals. Instead, I hope you will use it over and over again until it is ragged and tattered. I hope you will find that it becomes one of the most useful tools you have to stimulate conversations and reduce assumptions about who does what.
>
> **WARNING!**

It would be easy if an appendix of this manual had the answers so that you could skip to the end and emerge, victorious and smiling, with all the "right" answers firmly in hand.

Don't skip to the last page to find the answers. They aren't there, although what you will find is a helpful test to open lines of communication.

Therefore, I'd recommend that you revisit the chapters, charts, and appendix test often. If you'll schedule a conversation as board and staff leaders at the beginning of each new leadership term, you'll reduce assumptions and clarify roles and responsibilities of both critical team leaders.

So, let's get to it!

To Recap

◆ The Invisible Yellow Line is the metaphorical division between the things the board is concerned with and the things the staff is concerned with.

◆ Adopting the Yellow Line terminology sets the stage for an honest discussion about roles.

◆ The Yellow Line may be repositioned to adapt to an organization emerging from its beginning stages to a more mature organization.

◆ The fundamentals of good governance still apply: Boards are responsible for strategic direction, policy, and fiscal oversight. Staffs are responsible for management and administration.

◆ The key to clarifying the roles at all levels of board and staff relationships is open and honest communications. That's what this manual is all about!

Chapter Two

The Invisible Yellow Line in Governance

IN THIS CHAPTER

···→ Ultimate governance authority and responsibilities of board members and the chief executive

···→ Basic governance duties of board members and the chief executive

···→ Fiduciary duties of care, loyalty, and honesty

···→ Bylaws, policies, and procedures

···→ Who can vote?

The Impact of the Yellow Line Today

Today more than ever, donors, regulators, and other stakeholders are holding nonprofits accountable for outcomes and achievements. Regulatory bodies are placing an increased emphasis on the governing body of the organization, requiring boards to operate more professionally. Boards are relying on their chief executives to ensure that knowledgeable and current management practices are in place to help them fulfill their roles of effective and efficient governance.

No organization can allow its board members to believe that being "just volunteers" absolves them from legal and fiduciary responsibility. Staff members must provide the internal management and administrative policies and procedures that support good governance.

You can download the current Form 990 at www.irs.gov. The section on governance could stimulate a useful discussion at the board level about governance practices, board policies,

The federal government requires more and more from nonprofit organizations in fiscal oversight, transparency, and governance. Just review the changes in reporting requirements on the IRS Form 990 in recent years. I love to challenge board members by asking whether they've ever reviewed their organization's Form 990. All too often I get blank stares and sideways glances. Your board's effective and efficient governance is clearly reflected in your annual 990—or not.

WARNING!

review, and oversight, which is exactly the purpose of the form. Since the IRS Form 990 is apt to change from year to year, it is a good practice for the board's executive committee and chief executive (at least) to review the form annually before it is completed to ensure best governance practices are in place for board and staff.

Take some time to review the current IRS Form 990, and you'll quickly clarify its importance by reviewing what your nonprofit must report.

The Board's Role in Governance

The board is responsible for effective and efficient governance of the organization. Okay, you say, but what does this look like?

Sometimes the Invisible Yellow Line is difficult to define in governance practice. For example, how does the board *know* that organizational governing policies and procedures are current and compliant with all regulations? The current IRS Form 990 references a number of governance policies and procedures that every nonprofit should consider putting in place, including a conflict of interest policy and a whistle-blower policy as well as others. One way the board can satisfy this governance requirement is to ensure that qualified professionals are recruited for board positions and that these professionals agree—using an annual commitment letter—to provide pro bono oversight within their areas of professional expertise.

When qualified professionals sit on the board or on an advisory committee of the board, they can review and recommend revisions to governing policies and procedures.

Board Committee Authority and Accountability

It is rarely a good idea that any committee of the board, except for the executive committee of elected officers, has authority to commit the board to anything binding. This should be stated in the bylaws so that board members are clear about voting and signatory authority.

A board leader recently told me that her board was a "working board" because her organization didn't have staff to carry out the administrative functions. So, she claimed, her board didn't have governance and fiduciary responsibilities. Unfortunately, I have heard this too many times before. Your nonprofit board is a nonprofit board, subject to federal, state, and local regulations and requirements, regardless of whether board members consider themselves a working board, a policy-making board, or a governing board!

watch out!

Recently, as I was training a group on the roles and responsibilities of a nonprofit board and chief executive, a couple of board members shared that they had met with a competing organization's board president and chief executive earlier that week. They explained that they had held this meeting as part of their role as members of the strategic planning committee and had endorsed a collaborative agreement between the two organizations. Imagine the surprise of the other board members, the chair of that committee, and the chief executive! While their intentions were probably good, when these few board members acted outside of the committee structure and in the absence of a strategic initiative endorsed by all, it resulted in a contentious and argumentative session that derailed the afternoon.

stories from the real world

The case study in the sidebar is an example of making a muddy mess of the Invisible Yellow Line. Individual members of the board operated outside their authority and without endorsement of the board committee they represented and voted to endorse a collaborative agreement with another nonprofit.

If a committee isn't functioning appropriately, the board leader should determine the reason, appoint a new chair, or assist in other productive ways to get the committee back on track.

The Chief Executive's Role in Governance

Ultimately, the chief executive is responsible for effective and efficient management of the nonprofit organization, but the CEO has governance responsibilities as well. For example, the board will likely rely on the chief executive to have up-to-date internal policies and procedures in place. These policies should govern such key areas as human resources, finances, resource development, and more, such as grievance, whistle blowers, document retention and destruction, and fiscal controls.

The chief executive must ensure that these internal governing policies are reviewed and updated regularly to follow current legal rules and regulations. The CEO should calendar professional reviews of the internal governing policies every three to five years to ensure compliance and discuss them with appropriate members of the board.

The Invisible Yellow Line in Fiduciary Duties

Boards of directors should be covered by directors and officers liability insurance (D&O insurance). Members should know what the policy covers and what it does not. In essence, a D&O policy is in place to protect the personal and professional assets of a board member and to cover the cost of hiring legal defense should the board or an individual member be sued. This coverage assumes that individuals and the board as a whole do not betray any of the three "duties" to follow.

There are three duties that govern the board: the duties of care, loyalty, and honesty.

principle

These three duties are likely to be found in every directors and officers liability policy and every book on board governance, and they are taught by every nonprofit board consultant. Although the titles may vary somewhat, the basic duties are the same.

The Duty of Care

The duty of care is usually stated, "Board members should act in good faith with the care that an ordinarily prudent person would exercise under similar circumstances."

The Board's Role in the Duty of Care

Board members should come to meetings prepared, having read pertinent materials in advance, and be ready to ask questions to clarify understanding before they vote on issues.

Board members can vote to *approve* the minutes of the previous meeting if they were at the meeting and can attest to the accuracy of the minutes. A board member can vote to *accept* the treasurer's report because the board member is relying on the treasurer to present a fair and accurate review of the finances, even though the board member has not personally reviewed all the cancelled checks and other financial materials.

Board members must support the actions and votes of the majority and not undermine the authority of the full board. Once the board has voted on a matter, a dissenting member has three options: First, ask the board to reconsider. If the board approves the option to revisit the issue, then the board sets a time to accomplish this and the dissenting member presents further arguments. Second, if the board declines, the dissenting member must find a way to support the decision. The last option is to resign from the board.

The Chief Executive's Role in the Duty of Care

The chief executive provides documents and materials to the board in advance of board meetings that will allow the board to come to

A nonprofit health-related foundation had the opportunity to purchase a large historic building for its offices. The building required considerable costly renovation. Some members of the board argued that this was not mission driven and that its funds should be used to support health-related efforts only. Others on the board argued that the building was a sound investment. After considerable discussion, the majority of the board voted to invest in the building.

Normally, no one outside the organization would have known about this issue. However, dissenting members of the board were on the evening news and in the daily newspaper expressing their dissatisfaction with the decision. You might agree that these dissenting board members betrayed their duty of care.

 **stories from the real world**

meetings prepared to act. The CEO's report to the board details strategic management issues that inform the board about the achievement of goals and any issues that require the board's review or require a board decision.

The Duty of Loyalty

The duty of loyalty means board members must put the interests of the organization first, above personal or professional interests.

Consider this: Does your organization have a banking relationship with the bank of which a board member is an officer? This is common, so a best practice is to put all your organization's vendor relationships out to bid every three to five years. This includes professional services, insurance, supplies, etc. This protects a board member from the appearance of personal or professional gain (private inurement). And it's just good business management to ensure that your organization is getting the highest benefit at the most reasonable cost. You can provide detail on this practice on the IRS Form 990.

The Board's Role in the Duty of Loyalty

Every board member must be aware of and disclose actual or perceived conflicts of interest. Your board should have a conflict of interest policy in place. Individual board members should sign their conflict of interest statements annually.

The Chief Executive's and Key Staff's Role in the Duty of Loyalty

The chief executive and other key staff members should also sign conflict of interest statements annually, disclosing any conflict or potential conflict. You should discuss with all staff members how your organization defines conflict of interest between staff members, between staff and board, and between staff and volunteers.

> Remember to update your conflict of interest statement annually to reflect the current IRS Form 990 definition of conflict of interest or independence.
>
>  practical tip

I recommend that you keep your conflict of interest form simple and succinct. Update the statement of required disclosures annually to reflect the current IRS Form 990 definition. A sample conflict of interest statement is included in **Appendix E**. Not only will signing the conflict of interest form annually serve as a reminder of conflicts that should be disclosed, but it will also make it easier to complete the required disclosures on the annual IRS Form 990.

The Duty of Honesty

The duty of honesty means that board members must act in accordance with the organization's stated mission and applicable laws, including bylaws.

Here are some examples of how difficult it might be to clarify conflict of interest. A board member sells insurance, and staff members purchase from him. A board member sells jewelry, and staff members purchase from her. A board member provides mediation and counseling, and staff members use her services to deal with internal agency issues. The Invisible Yellow Line in these instances may be clear to some but not to others, which is why communication is so critical to prevent confusion.

watch out!

The Board's Role in the Duty of Honesty

Your board holds primary responsibility for ensuring that your organization follows and complies with all local, state, and federal nonprofit regulations and reporting.

In addition, your board must ensure mission-driven decision making in its strategic discussion about programs, services, resource development, etc. It is a best practice for every organization to schedule a formal review of its mission every three to five years, at least. I recommend that a mission review should be a part of every organization's annual planning retreat.

Your board should not rely on someone else to prepare the entire IRS Form 990. Review and discuss *at least* the governance portions with your executive committee, and include a general review of the governance sections with the full board. At a minimum, the board should know what this important report says about its governance practices since the Form 990 is a public document.

Your board should be aware of critical dates and deadlines and be sure they are met. As a board member, do you know the deadline for the annual IRS Form 990? Answer: it is due to the IRS on the fifteenth day of the fifth month after the end of your fiscal year. Equally important is complying with local and state regulations that govern nonprofits. The board is ultimately responsible, even if it doesn't complete the required documentation, so bookmark important filing dates on your board calendar.

Print your organization's mission on all board and committee meeting agendas to reinforce its importance in decision making. Encourage people to challenge discussions and decisions as to whether they will have a high impact on the mission or whether there is mission drift.

 practical tip

The Chief Executive's and Key Staff's Role in the Duty of Honesty

The board will delegate much of the actual regulatory compliance to key staff. It is the staff's responsibility to inform the board about important regulatory deadlines and show that they have been met. The chief executive ensures that internal organizational policies and procedures are reviewed regularly and are legal and current. Further, the CEO keeps the mission and purpose alive and vibrant in all organizational operations.

Governing Documents

As required by the duty of honesty, your board must follow its bylaws. I am often asked for advice about how to handle a particular board governance issue, and my immediate response is usually, "I don't know how you should handle this issue specifically. What do your bylaws say?" Inevitably, the answer can be found there.

Let's talk a minute about bylaws versus policies and procedures. Bylaws are your *governing document*, not your *operating document*.

I recommend that you allow some level of flexibility in your bylaws. If you do, it makes changing and adapting them much easier without going through the usually arduous process of amending them.

For example, state the number of members of the board as "no less than (number) or more than (number)" to allow your board to recruit the best and most appropriate people to serve rather than meet the desired number with anybody whose breath fogs the mirror! Conform to the current IRS regulations and check with your state's regulatory agency for nonprofits to determine the minimum number required.

> Bylaws are the governing document that defines the *what* of governance, such as organizational purpose, board membership, roles and duties, voting requirements, meetings, and the like. A board operating policy manual lays out the nitty-gritty procedures of **how** your board operates, such as what constitutes an excused absence, how checks are signed, and other day-to-day board administrative issues.
>
> finition

Your bylaws should also list *only* those standing committees that are absolutely required to govern effectively, e.g., executive and nominating committee. State that "the president (or chair) of the board has the authority to appoint committees that are required to carry out the annual plan of work." This prevents having committees simply for the sake of having committees.

What if the board is operating in ways not in line with the bylaws? For example, if the bylaws state an attendance requirement for board members but this requirement is not followed or is inconsistently followed, the board is not governing properly.

If a board member is consistently absent or has violated the attendance requirements as stated in the bylaws, the board leader should address the issue immediately, require active participation, or allow the absentee board member to resign per the requirement of the bylaws.

A best practice is for the board leader to appoint a task force every three to five years to review bylaws and recommend what changes, if any, are required as defined in the amendment section of the bylaws.

A few years ago, I was invited to join the board of a long-standing nonprofit in my community. As part of my due diligence, I asked to review a copy of the bylaws. After an uncomfortable few moments, the chief executive admitted he wasn't sure where a copy could be found, but he promised to look into it for me. And he did, proudly sharing a copy of the bylaws—typewritten! I am serious. They hadn't been reviewed in years. I will admit that I declined the offer to join the board.

stories from the real world

But how does the board know the *how* of governing? For example, if the bylaws allow a board member to have a specific number of excused absences per year, how does the board member get excused from a meeting?

Here is where a board operating policy manual comes into play. This document describes *how* the board operates. It clarifies the governing rules and regulations and explains them in detail. For example, who has signature authority and for what; your expectations of time, talent, and treasure; what constitutes an excused absence from a board meeting; how you conduct regular board business; how you handle conflicts of interest; chain of command; and so on.

The policy manual can be updated more easily than bylaws and can be amended to reflect changes in the board's day-to-day operations.

The Invisible Yellow Line—Who Can Vote?

This is another issue that has Yellow Line implications and will be defined, in most instances, in bylaws. Under normal circumstances, appointed members of an advisory, honorary, or emeritus board will not have voting authority.

The Board's Role in Voting

Most boards operate with an executive committee of elected officers of the board (the leader, leader-elect, past leader, secretary, and treasurer). The executive committee can act as a filter for the board, ensuring the full board gets the information it requires to govern effectively. The executive committee usually has the power defined in the bylaws to act on behalf of the full board, allowing for flexibility in addressing critical or time-sensitive matters. Usually, the chief executive is an ex officio nonvoting member of this committee.

The Chief Executive's Role in Voting

The chief executive is hired by the board, reports to the board, serves as an advisor to the board, and should not have voting authority at the board level.

Review and Clarify the Invisible Yellow Line in Your Governance Practices

This worksheet will help you clarify your organization's Invisible Yellow Line in governance. You might complete it individually and then share the results to start a conversation about how you will define the Invisible Yellow Line in the context of your organization. The Yellow Line is invisible—but it can move from time to time as situations might demand. For example, a board member steps across the Yellow Line when asked to share professional advice in the member's area of expertise. The important thing to remember is that there are not always "right" answers in terms of the line's location. Just start the discussion by using this worksheet to avoid assumptions and confusion.

Discuss the key activity and decide for your organization who has primary responsibility at this time: board, board leader, chief executive, or other staff member. Or is it a shared responsibility?

The Invisible Yellow Line in Governance

Key Activity	Responsibility
Who has ultimate responsibility for effective and efficient governance?	
Who ensures that board committees have clearly defined limits on their authority?	
Who reviews the annual IRS Form 990 before it is filed?	
Who is covered by and abides by directors and officers liability insurance?	
Who understands and abides by the duty of care?	
Who comes to meetings prepared to act, having reviewed pertinent materials in advance?	
Who reviews internal governance policies regularly to ensure they comply with current regulations?	
Who respects the actions of the majority and does not undermine its joint authority?	
Who understands and abides by the duty of loyalty?	
Who ensures that the board has diversity in skills but does not advance personal interests?	
Who signs annual conflict of interest statements, disclosing potential conflicts as defined by the current IRS Form 990?	
Who ensures that policies are in place to manage conflicts of interest?	
Who ensures that conflict of interest statements are revised annually to reflect the IRS Form 990 definitions?	
Who understands and abides by the duty of honesty?	

Key Activity	Responsibility
Who ensures compliance with all federal, state, and local laws and requirements?	
Who ensures that the mission statement is reviewed regularly and revised as required?	
Who is responsible to ensure that mission-driven decision making is enforced at all levels?	
Who manages day-to-day compliance with internal policies and procedures and reports to regulatory bodies?	
Who ensures that bylaws allow for flexibility in board size and number of committees?	
Who reviews bylaws every three to five years and revises if required?	
Who develops an operating policy and procedure manual?	
Who enforces meeting attendance requirements consistently, as defined in the bylaws?	
Who attends board meetings as an advisor and is not a voting member of the board?	
Who has voting authority in governance matters?	
Who has oversight responsibility for governance policies and procedures?	

To Recap

◆ The board holds the ultimate responsibility for effective and efficient governance of the organization.

◆ The chief executive supports the board's effective governance by providing information and feedback.

◆ Board members must understand and abide by the duties of care, loyalty, and honesty.

◆ The chief executive ensures that internal governance policies are reviewed and revised regularly for legality and compliance.

◆ The board and CEO govern strategically to ensure the organization serves and meets its mission.

Chapter Three

The Invisible Yellow Line in Management

IN THIS CHAPTER

--→ Board and staff roles and responsibilities

--→ Meetings, meetings, meetings

--→ Self evaluations

--→ Getting new people on the same page

--→ Thanking, recognizing, and rewarding

Both board and staff have key responsibility to take advantage of the time, talent, and treasure of your organization's management and volunteer resources. This chapter will discuss best practices in everything from meetings to minutes, evaluations to burnout. In some circumstances, overlap can occur in organizational management, especially when it comes to oversight. These are times when clarifying the Invisible Yellow Line is especially important to prevent assumptions and frustration.

Drawing the Line

Essentially, the board manages the board and the chief executive, and the chief executive manages the staff and the day-to-day administration of the organization.

From time to time, the Invisible Yellow Line in management can be blurred. For example, the chief executive might involve the board financial professional in establishing and reviewing fiscal policies, or a board human resource professional in staff grievance or discipline activities. Or a board member might volunteer to spend time in the office supporting clerical functions.

As a board member, I once volunteered to help the small staff of an organization build and update its donor database, which I did at the organization's office. From time to time, I would hear conversations between staff members that I felt I shouldn't hear and had to remind the staff that I was still a board member, not a staff member, and that they should hold those conversations elsewhere. If a board member overhears and gets involved in staff issues, that board member has seriously crossed over the Invisible Yellow Line!

watch out!

In these instances, ground rules for the Yellow Line have to be clarified and board volunteers need to remember which hat you are wearing when you are involved in organizational management functions. You'll need to focus on the task at hand and not get involved in the day-to-day management, which is the chief executive's responsibility.

This is especially difficult when everyone is friendly and there are fewer barriers to communication and interaction. It takes discipline on the part of the board and the chief executive to keep communication open without crossing the Invisible Yellow Line.

Meetings, Meetings, Meetings

Meetings are the meat and potatoes of most organizations' operations. They can be exciting or dreadfully dull. They can be focused on actions and outcomes or monumental wastes of valuable resources. Do you ever wonder who replaced all your bright and energetic board or staff members with the half-asleep zombies you see sitting around you? Both sides of the Invisible Yellow Line can adopt the ideas below to take full advantage of the board's and staff's valuable time and talent.

Here are some practical tips for improving your organization's meetings. A good way to define the Invisible Yellow Line in meetings might be to review this entire section with incoming board leaders every year, setting clear expectations about whose role it is to set the agenda, send meeting announcements, take minutes, and the like. This is often where the roles of board and staff will be different (they might move) from year to year to accommodate the preferences of your organization's leaders.

Practical improvements to your meetings can change board and staff from zombies to energized, enthusiastic participants.

 **practical tip**

Be Prepared

Board meetings: send agenda, minutes, financial reports, chief executive report, and committee reports to all board members in advance of the meeting. Usually the staff supports the board leader in distributing these materials. If a board member can't attend a meeting prepared to act (remember that duty of care?), ask this board member to abstain. Do *not* hold up the meeting to give a board member time to get caught up. This merely rewards the behavior you don't want, and before long, no one will come prepared. Leading the board meeting is the board leader's role, not the chief executive's.

Staff meetings: send agenda, reports, and other documents for the meeting in advance. Require staff members to come prepared so that they don't hold up the important work to be done. Under normal circumstances, board members should not attend staff meetings.

Be Timely

Board meetings: start meetings on time. If after fifteen minutes you don't have a quorum, the board leader should adjourn the meeting. The board can meet and discuss, but you can't vote without a quorum. Discuss this in board orientation and include this in your board policy manual.

A chief executive of a large nonprofit was surprised at a routine staff meeting when two members of the board appeared to attend the meeting. The chief executive was, rightfully, uncomfortable and felt threatened. As it turned out, a disgruntled staff member had taken it upon himself to invite his friends on the board to attend to "see for themselves" what went on! Clearly, the Invisible Yellow Line had been crossed by several team members.

 stories from the real world

Board and staff meetings: end meetings on time unless there is a valid reason to go over the agreed-upon time limit. When setting the meeting agenda, if there is an issue that will require a longer time commitment than usual, the board or staff leader should alert participants *in advance* so they can plan accordingly and won't have to leave the meeting in the middle of an important discussion.

Be Organized

Board meetings: if the board leader knows *in advance* that there will not be a quorum, alert all board members that the meeting is cancelled or postponed in plenty of time so that board members can use that time elsewhere. While this may not appear to be directly applicable to the Invisible Yellow Line, it is worth including in this manual as a matter of courtesy and communication.

A board often found that it could not act due to a lack of a quorum at its regular meetings. So the board leader assigned the organization's chief executive the task of contacting every board member before every meeting to remind them to attend. I would strongly argue that this is not the job of the chief executive or a member of the organization's staff! Rather, this is the responsibility of the board leader or board secretary.

watch out!

One last thought here. Last time I looked, board and staff members are adults. Since regular board and staff meetings are scheduled at the beginning of the year, there should be no need for phone calls or emails to remind people. You need to hold these adults accountable.

Move the Business Along

Certainly, every board and staff meeting should follow an agenda, sent out in advance, as we previously discussed. Include not only the usual review of agenda, previous meeting minutes, and financials, but also a status check of the actions within the annual plan of work. Delegate committee discussions to committees. Otherwise, there exists the real temptation to micromanage committees, and that diminishes the work and authority of the committee itself.

Finally, I recommend using a modified form of *Robert's Rules of Order* to keep business moving along. I've included a simple list of parliamentary rules in **Appendix G**.

Minutes and the Invisible Yellow Line

While we are on the subject of who does what, I am going to stir up a hornet's nest. I certainly hope your chief executive or a staff person does not take minutes at board meetings. It is a *board meeting* after all, and that is the responsibility of the board secretary. I've often served as the board secretary and managed to take minutes and participate in the meeting as well, so I know it can be done.

Your board meeting minutes constitute the legal documentation of your board's actions and could be subpoenaed in case of a legal action. That is why it is important that the board *itself* take primary responsibility for recording its meeting minutes. Board meeting minutes are far too important to be delegated. The board secretary should sign the board meeting minutes. Since the chief executive attends board meetings as an advisor, it is not appropriate to delegate minutes to this person.

Board meeting minutes are considered permanent records and should not be deleted after a certain period.

How much detail should be included in minutes? Here's an easy test. Would the discussion at this meeting be of interest to the local investigative reporter? If so, include sufficient detail as a record that care was taken in the decision making.

Annual Board Self-Performance Evaluation

To keep abreast of best practices, your board should undertake a self-evaluation annually, assessing individual performance and board performance as a whole. Again, this is the board's responsibility, so this should be directed by the board leader, not the chief executive.

The Board's Role in New-Member Orientation

The best boards require orientation for all new board members, ideally before the new members' first board meeting. The orientation should be facilitated by the board leader. You might include the treasurer to explain financial statements.

What should be included in board orientation? At minimum:

◆ Mission, vision, and organization statistics

◆ Review of board job description, conflict of interest statement, and clear and honest expectations of time, talent, and treasure

◆ Review of basic governance, fiscal, and financial responsibilities, and how to read monthly financial statements

◆ Overview of bylaws and the board policy manual, with emphasis on *how* the board operates and the bylaws' governing rules

◆ Overview of the strategic plan and how to get involved in a board committee

◆ Organization chart for board and staff, and introduction to leadership staff members

◆ Critical agency policies such as grievance, whistle blower, and others that might involve the board at some point

◆ Review of organization: history, key programs and services, and outcomes and results

◆ Tour or high-impact impression of *why* your organization exists (a testimonial from a client works well if a tour is not appropriate). New board members should leave the orientation with a story to tell that reinforces *why* they joined the board in the first place.

> Prior to a strategic planning session I facilitated, the board leader asked for time for a brief board meeting. A brand-new board member was there for her first meeting. She appeared somewhat lost when the board leader rushed through minutes of the previous meeting and the financial report. But, to her immense credit, when asked to accept the treasurer's report, she had the courage to speak up and ask for explanations of a couple of the numbers as shown. Unfortunately, the board leader appeared exasperated and did not answer her questions thoroughly. Had there been ample time allotted in new-member orientation, these questions could have been answered.

 **stories from the real world**

The Staff's Role in New-Board-Member Orientation

The chief executive should play an active role in orientation of new board members. The CEO will provide the basic organizational information, history, overview of programs and services, operational policies and procedures, and other internal information a new board member needs to know about how your organization operates. The chief financial officer (CFO) may want to be involved in a discussion of finances. Key staff members can present insights about key organizational programs and services.

Orientation: Getting New Staff Members on the Same Page

New-staff-member orientation is just as important as new-board-member orientation. Clearly, there are detailed policies and procedures that will affect how well your staff manages the day-to-day operations of your organization. Even if the new staff member is experienced in the role, everyone has to be oriented into the *how* and *why* of your particular operation.

The Chief Executive's Role in Staff Orientation

The CEO ensures that every new member of the staff receives an orientation program similar to what the board receives, with an emphasis on internal operational management policies and procedures. Depending on the new staff person's job, the staff person might need to sign a conflict of interest statement and/or a confidentiality statement. Staff members will need a tour and an understanding of the entire scope of your organization.

In **Chapter One**, we discussed the importance of the leader's role in setting the tone for the collaborative partnership between board and staff. Leaders can demonstrate this collaboration when they explain each party's respective role to new staff and board members.

practical tip

The Board's Role in Staff Orientation

The board leader or representative might attend a part of new-staff-member orientation to introduce the board's role in governance and oversight.

The Yellow Line in Keeping Performance High

You Will Get What You Accept and What You Reward.

This statement holds true with children, with employees, with spouses or significant others, with business partners, and even with boards of directors and staff members.

Here's how this works for the board: if it's okay for some board members, but not others, to make annual contributions, those who *do* give will likely stop giving before long.

If it's okay to hold up the start of board meetings for late-comers or no-shows who haven't called in advance, how long will it be before those who make the effort to be on time stop doing so?

If it's okay for some board members to stay on the board because they give money but don't attend meetings, what message does this send about the importance of governance and high standards?

It is the board leader's, not the chief executive's, job to manage the board. Some boards will place this responsibility on a governance committee, or the executive committee, or the board leader. Responsibility for board management must be clearly defined in the board's policy manual to make clear who has ultimate responsibility. But board members ultimately report to the board leader. I have seen this role delegated to the chief executive,

The squeaky wheel gets the grease means *you will get what you accept and what you reward.*

important

which is unfair. Managing the board can easily place the chief executive in a compromising position, both legally and professionally, and it blurs the Invisible Yellow Line.

Here's how it works for staff: if it's okay for some staff members, but not others, to come and go within agreed-upon hours, how long before the others are resentful? If it's perceived that some staff members get special attention because they complain about things, how long before others start complaining? Again, it is the chief executive's job to manage the organization's staff. However, there can be times when the Invisible Yellow Line can move and board professionals might be called upon to assist the chief executive—for example, using their expertise in human resources issues or fiscal controls. In these instances, it is important that the board member step in when called upon and then step away from getting involved further in the organization's day-to-day management. If you fall into the trap of paying more attention to the problem board member or staff person and taking the others for granted, how long before the high performers feel resentful, neglected, and overlooked?

If you think about it, the old adage about the squeaky wheel is so true! We often reward the behavior we *don't want* and take the other behaviors for granted. So this brings us to the next topic: thanking.

Thank You, Merci, Danke, Gracias

If we stop rewarding the behavior we *don't* want, we have to reward the behavior we *do* want. You probably can't say thank you enough. The Invisible Yellow Line can blur somewhat in these examples. Of course, the board leader should recognize board members' exceptional performance and should do the same for the chief executive. The board leader might also attend a staff celebration to show the support of the board for the organization's achievements.

Here are important things to remember when recognizing and thanking both board and staff members:

- ◆ It's got to be timely. If a board member does something wonderful in March and you wait until the board's annual meeting in October, that's just insulting.

- ◆ It's got to be meaningful. While it might be easier for the board leader to ask the chief executive to create a lovely certificate or get a plaque made, that is usually not particularly meaningful to the recipient. Ask someone who knows the board or staff member well what would be meaningful. It doesn't have to be

> If a staff person overperforms on an assignment and the action is not recognized right away, what message does it send? Thank staff members when the action occurs. Send a handwritten note of thanks. Make a big deal in the office with bells and whistles (literally). Recognize good behavior at the next general staff meeting. Board members, too, who overperform should similarly be recognized. Board members are people too!

important

expensive. It has to be *meaningful*. Remember that the chief executive is not the board leader's personal assistant, so be cautious when delegating details of board recognition.

◆ Thank those who make it possible for board members to be board members. Thank secretaries and administrative assistants. Thank spouses or partners. Be creative.

> ### Meaningful Thanking
>
> I once gave a certificate for a year's worth of fancy dog treats to a board member who loved her dog. The board member was thrilled, and the dog was happy too.
>
>

Do I Smell Smoke? Identifying and Dealing with Burnout in Board and Staff

Is the board room getting smoky? Are some board members getting burned out? Often, burned-out board members are the last to smell the smoke and are consumed with guilt because they can't fulfill the obligations of being an active member of the board.

The Role of the Board Leader in Managing Board Member Burnout

An annual board member commitment letter is a critical tool for your organization's board of directors. The board leader should take responsibility for presenting the commitment letter to every board member. It should be completed annually so board members can reassess their commitment to the organization because all too often, life gets in the way of volunteering.

> The board leader should not assign responsibility for chasing delinquent board members to the chief executive or another staff person. It bears repeating: the board leader manages the board.
>
> **watch out!**

An escape clause at the end of the commitment letter creates an understanding that it is okay to resign before a term is up or when the board member can't be active or fulfill the commitment. Commitment letters are returned to the board leader, not the chief executive or other staff person, for filing in the board's permanent records. If a board member does not sign and return the commitment letter, it is the board leader's responsibility to follow up directly with the board member, discussing whether or not the board member is ready to recommit or whether it is time to resign.

Another good use of the annual commitment letter is to renew every board member's commitment to making an annual personal meaningful financial contribution. You will see on the sample commitment letter in

> An annual board member commitment letter creates a culture of understanding that sometimes life gets in the way of volunteering and gives a board member a way out without guilt or embarrassment.
>
> practical tip

Appendix B a place for the board member to commit to an amount. If the commitment isn't realized, the board leader should address the issue with the individual board member so the goal of 100 percent annual giving isn't compromised. Again, this responsibility cannot be delegated to the chief executive.

The Role of the Chief Executive in Managing Staff Burnout

Burnout happens. It happens to volunteers and it happens to staff. Far too often, we make the assumption that if we just paid staff more, it would solve everything. It has been my experience that simply recognizing burnout before our staff member is reduced to ashes goes a long way to putting out the fire. Your organization's chief executive should be allowed the leeway to deal creatively with potential staff burnout. Give paid time off. Listen and understand the issues. Consider a job shift if possible. Be willing to compromise to keep exceptional staff or help an exceptional staff person transition to another organization.

Ideas for the Board Leader and Chief Executive to Reenergize Burned-Out Board and Staff

Here are some ideas that the board leader and chief executive can use to reenergize burned-out board or staff, as the case may be.

Reinvest in Mission and Purpose

◆ Board members can reenergize by touring the organization's facilities. Staff members can present significant achievements to the board.

◆ Invite clients to present achievements at board or staff meetings.

◆ Print your organization's mission and vision on all meeting agendas.

◆ Report on statistics, outcomes, and accomplishments at every board or staff meeting to build a sense of accomplishment and pride.

A board leader once complained to me that she couldn't count on board members to attend meetings regularly, get involved in committees, or make annual financial contributions, even after she nagged and nagged. After we talked about the issue, she realized that her board members were exhibiting classic symptoms of burnout, so she asked them what was needed to reaffirm and reenergize them. It was pretty easy—they had lost touch with the reasons they had committed in the first place and needed to reinvest.

The same story can be told about staff members who exhibit symptoms of burnout and boredom. Often, all that is needed is a way to reinvest in the importance of their jobs and where they fit in the organization.

stories from the real world

Ask and Listen

◆ Ask: Why are you a part of this organization? What do you want to accomplish?

◆ Ask: What would make you feel valued?

◆ Ask: How we can reengage you and help you use your talents more effectively?

Put the Pieces Together

◆ Involve both board and key staff in the annual planning retreat to set annual goals.

◆ Report on accomplishments at every board and staff meeting.

◆ Hold everyone accountable for achieving goals.

◆ Communicate, communicate, communicate—in a variety of ways and as often as possible—to keep board and staff engaged.

Have Fun

Hold occasional social events that include board, staff, families, clients, and other volunteers. This is a time when the Invisible Yellow Line might disappear completely and everyone is focused on the greater purpose of your organization.

Value and Appreciate

◆ Thank board and staff members regularly and often.

◆ Personalize thanking and recognition of both board and staff so it is meaningful.

◆ Put it in print. Recognize board and staff accomplishments in your newsletter, the newspaper, and your website.

◆ Feature "Board Member of the Month" and "Staff Person of the Month" in your organization's newsletter, website, or community newspaper. Send photos, letters of support, recognition of achievement, etc.

Bless and Release

◆ Use annual commitment letters to allow board members to resign with dignity.

As a board leader, I have always used annual commitment letters as a way to show that I understand how real life can get in the way of volunteering at times. Every single time I have allowed a board member to resign after not receiving the signed commitment letter, the response from the board member has been "Thank you. I felt so guilty. I appreciate your understanding." Often, the resigning board member has found other, less taxing ways to support the organization.

stories from the real world

◆ Provide for a guilt-free exit for board volunteers and staff members.

◆ Reassign tired board members to new opportunities.

◆ Reassign tired staff members to new opportunities, if only for a brief period of time.

For the Board: the Importance of Term Limits

It is a best practice critical to your organization's success that regular turnover of board members occurs to generate new ideas, new enthusiasm, new contacts, new relationships, and new leadership. Your board's bylaws should include term limits to accomplish this turnover in a graduated manner so that not all board members leave at once when terms expire.

The average I have seen after reading lots of bylaws is a three-year term that is renewable once. Here is an important point: the second term is not guaranteed. It should be earned by showing exceptional commitment and demonstrations of time, talent, and treasure.

It is the board leader's responsibility to clarify expectations to all board members at new-board-member orientation and when terms are expiring. Many boards include these expectations in the board policy manual (discussed at new-board-member orientation). They should state that board members will attend meetings prepared to act, make annual financial contributions, serve actively on board committees, and avoid conflicts of interest. They should also make clear any other service expectations for board members.

> Term limits provide for new ideas, new energy, and new leadership. Board members should not serve for life, regardless of how good they are. Use term limits to renew and revitalize your board and retire exceptional board members to advisory or emeritus status to recognize their contributions.
>
>
> **! important**

Okay, right now, I hear you protesting that you have some great board members that you don't want to lose after six years. Allow me to challenge this thinking. Why do you think you will lose these valuable volunteers? You won't! If board members are truly committed to your organization, they will find other ways to support the mission when their terms expire. They can serve on committees. They can volunteer in other capacities. They won't have to spend their valuable volunteer time in board meetings but can redirect their energy to other ways to serve your organization. It is the board leader's responsibility to assess each board member's commitment annually and to offer alternatives when a term expires.

If your bylaws specify term limits, and they should, follow them consistently. You can't let GOB (Good Old Bob) go when his term expires but pretend term limits don't apply to GGB (Great and Good Betty) and keep her on the board past the end of her prescribed term. GOB is the board member who comes late to meetings or not at all, asks questions that have already been answered, isn't prepared, and interferes with the work of committees. On the other hand, GGB is the board member who makes every effort to be on time, is prepared, offers sound advice, and sets the example for others with an annual contribution. The board leader should deal with GOB and recognize and reward GGB, but GGB must exit the board at the end of her term too.

Review and Clarify the Invisible Yellow Line in Your Organizational Management

This worksheet will help you clarify the Invisible Yellow Line for management in your organization. You might complete it individually and then share the results to start a conversation about how you will define the Invisible Yellow Line to operate most effectively and efficiently. The Yellow Line is invisible and it moves. Each organization might define its position differently. The important thing to remember is that there are not always "right" answers. Just open the lines of communication using this worksheet to avoid assumptions and confusion.

Discuss the key activity and decide for your organization who has primary responsibility at this time: board, board leader, chief executive, or other staff member. Or is it a shared responsibility?

The Invisible Yellow Line in Organizational Management

Key Activity	Responsibility
Who schedules regular meetings at the beginning of the year?	
Who ensures that meetings are useful, informative, and well attended?	
Who is responsible for sending meeting materials to participants in advance?	
Who ensures that meetings begin on time and usually last about one hour?	
Who plans for extra time at meetings in advance when the agenda requires it?	
Who is responsible to ensure that a quorum is achieved at all meetings?	
Who attends meetings without reminders?	
Who ensures that committee work is delegated to committees?	
Who does not micromanage committees?	
Who makes sure that meeting leaders use basic parliamentary procedure?	
Who takes minutes at board meetings?	
Who ensures that minutes of board meetings include appropriate levels of detail?	

Key Activity	Responsibility
Who is responsible for ensuring that board meeting minutes are retained forever?	
Who signs board meeting minutes?	
Who engages in an annual self-evaluation process?	
Who is responsible for orienting new board members before their first board meeting?	
Who requires new staff members to attend orientation?	
Who recognizes, thanks, and rewards the best behaviors?	
Who recognizes burnout and deals with it proactively?	
Who signs an annual commitment letter?	
Who ensures that term limits are in place and enforced consistently?	
Who honors and recognizes exemplary retiring board members?	

To Recap

◆ Board and staff roles and responsibilities can sometimes overlap in key management functions. It is important to clarify expectations for board and staff.

◆ Meetings can be time wasters or can be productive, energetic, and useful.

◆ Annual evaluations are important for both board and staff to keep people focused and on track.

◆ New-member orientation is the key in getting new people on the same page.

◆ Do you smell smoke? Deal with burnout creatively in both board and staff.

◆ Thank and recognize exceptional performance.

Chapter Four

The Invisible Yellow Line in Financial Operations

IN THIS CHAPTER

- ---→ Board and staff roles in financial management

- ---→ Financial oversight

- ---→ Budgeting

- ---→ Fiscal controls

Increasingly, donors, grantors, and regulatory bodies are scrutinizing how a nonprofit organization manages its fiscal responsibilities and the nonprofit's transparency in regard to financial operations. You want to make sure you are proactive, rather than reactive, in this respect. For example, you might post your current IRS Form 990 on your website as a demonstration of this intention of transparency.

The Board's Role in Financial Oversight

In most nonprofit organizations, the board treasurer and the executive committee take the lead in fiscal oversight, but it is the ultimate responsibility of the full board to ensure sound financial management, including appropriate oversight, separation of duties, independent reviews and audits, and so on.

Of course, the board should review financial reports at every meeting. The executive committee or budget and finance committee or board treasurer should review the detailed report prior to presenting an overview to the full board. And the board should ensure that adequate internal procedures are in place to prevent malfeasance or fraud at any level.

Okay, I am embarrassed, but I will share an incident that happened to me as the new member of a board several years ago. I asked if an audit had been done and was told that it was just "too expensive." Red flag! Warning! Unfortunately, I remained on the board, diligently reviewing the rather superficial financial reports each month as presented by a chief executive everyone loved and trusted. You can anticipate the end of this story. Indeed, the financial reports showed that checks had been written to pay the bills but, unfortunately, were not mailed. By the time the board realized the extent of the problem, the organization was nearly $100,000 in debt!

stories from the real world

Note: this clearly emphasizes the need to recruit and retain qualified financial professionals on the board and the importance of budgeting for an annual independent audit or review.

What the full board needs to review each month is budget compared with actual figures. The board should set an amount for any variances above or below the budget that require a written explanation. If the shortfall is significant, the board should hold immediate strategic discussions about how the variance might affect programs and services and what should be done to ensure your organization's mission does not suffer as a result.

The Staff's Role in Financial Oversight

The chief executive or chief financial officer monitors the day-to-day revenue and expenditures, noting *in advance* of the board meeting any deficit that might have a significant impact on your organization's programs and services, then alerting the board and presenting alternatives. Any significant deficit should be shared immediately with the board leadership so the potential consequences of the deficit can be averted or minimized.

In addition, the chief executive and key staff should undertake a cost/benefit analysis of every program, service, and fundraising activity for outcomes and cost effectiveness and be willing to recommend changes as a result. These analyses can be shared with appropriate board committees or the full board as part of the annual planning meeting.

Fiscal transparency and controls are more important than ever for every nonprofit. How does your organization stack up in light of today's environment and expectations?

food for thought

Budgeting

Often, annual budgets are increased by a simple percentage to account for increased costs of doing business, but does this really afford a comprehensive review of critical expenses and revenue? Perhaps not, and this process can result in upwardly spiraling costs without a careful review of efficiencies to be found and implemented.

Perhaps a better way to ensure a feasible annual budget is to commit the organization to a zero-based budget exercise every few years. This assumes that nothing is in place and that the organization has just begun and starts each budget section at zero. This requires thorough and careful research into best and efficient practices.

The budget should support your annual strategic goals and action plans and should be understood and "owned" by both the board and staff leadership.

The Staff's Role in Budgeting

Usually, the chief executive drafts the annual budget and then presents it to the board's executive committee or finance committee for detailed review before presenting it to the full board. Of course, getting input from other staff leaders is important because it strengthens their sense of ownership of the budget and goals.

It is the chief executive's responsibility to establish and ensure the staff salaries and benefits are fair and equitable.

The Board's Role in Budgeting

Although the budget may be developed by the chief executive, ultimately the board has the responsibility for ensuring it is realistic, adequate, and attainable.

Far too often, board members merely rely on the projections from the staff without carefully reviewing the budget both from an expense and a revenue perspective.

A best practice for the board is ensuring the budget has a reserve of three to six months of operating funds.

The board should not be involved in setting salaries and benefits for any staff member other than the chief executive. The board approves an aggregate amount in the budget for staff salaries and benefits.

According to the current IRS Form 990, the board should carefully review extemporaneous and comparative data when establishing the chief executive's salary and benefits. To accomplish this, there are many salary and benefit surveys available. You can find them on the Internet by searching for "nonprofit salary survey."

important

Fiscal Controls

Staff leadership and the board's financial officer should review written organizational fiscal policies and procedures every year. These policies should state who has authority to sign contracts over a certain amount, what should be reviewed by the board prior to signing, who signs checks over a particular amount, and how donations are processed. It should specify internal controls to prevent fraud, separation of receiving and recording cash and other contributions, who has signatory authority, how banking relationships are managed, and every other detail of financial management. For example, the person who reconciles bank statements should never have signatory authority. This simple practice, even in small organizations, serves to remove the temptation to defraud.

Other policies that are critical to fiscal management include a board-endorsed written investment policy and a gift acceptance policy that clarifies what tangible and intangible donations your organization will and will not accept. You can find good examples of these policies by searching the Internet.

> Nonprofits are certainly not immune to embezzlement and fraud. Be sure your organization has the internal controls in place to prevent this from happening. Both board advisors and staff leaders "own" this responsibility.
>
>
> **important**

Additionally, an important fiscal policy should state who has authority to sign contracts and documents for the organization and at what monetary level.

An annual independent audit or independent cash review is essential to most organizations and is often required by certain funders. Far too many organizations have been negligent in this arena because it can be an expensive item in the budget. Unsuspecting boards may then be caught off guard when a trusted employee commits fraud or embezzles funds. Although we may want to believe that the nonprofit sector is immune to fraud, in fact there are many nonprofits, both large and small, that have suffered fraud. The responsibility for ensuring adequate fiscal controls ultimately resides with the board but is usually delegated to the chief executive to manage.

The Board's Role in Fiscal Controls

The board provides oversight and is ultimately responsible for assuring stakeholders and regulators that your organization has appropriate fiscal controls in place and that you are in total compliance with federal and other regulations governing nonprofits.

It is critical that the board treasurer or another key board officer has the experience and expertise to review and ensure that internal fiscal controls are adequate and in place. The board leader is ultimately responsible for ensuring that someone on the board has this professional expertise or that it has contracted with the appropriate professional.

> When I was hired as the executive director of a statewide nonprofit, I was aware that the organization was close to losing its statewide charter from the national organization because so little money had been raised. I had a huge staff—composed of me and a sweet woman who answered the phones, paid the bills, and did the office work. It didn't take me long at all to uncover her scheme: changing the payee on checks to her own name. It wasn't even a sophisticated form of embezzlement, but it had been working for some time because people liked her and trusted her. The board and former chief executive had clearly not understood their ultimate Yellow Line and legal responsibilities.
>
> **watch out!**

The board should have adopted a whistle-blower policy that allows confidential reporting of any suspected or confirmed financial impropriety. The policy should prohibit retaliation and ensure adequate investigation and correction. If you don't have a whistle-blower policy, just Google it and you will find lots of examples.

The annual audit or financial review should be presented to the full board by the independent auditor or reviewer, not by a staff person. The board should agree to act on any credible findings revealed in the audit. These actions should be documented in the board meeting minutes. Having the audit presented by the independent source ensures fiscal separation and transparency. This should not be construed as mistrust of the chief executive. In fact, the chief executive should welcome this opportunity to present a positive outcome that ensures good fiscal management.

The Staff's Role in Fiscal Controls

The internal management and administrative functions of fiscal controls are the responsibility of the chief executive and leadership staff. Appropriate internal controls must be in place and must be reviewed regularly by the appropriate staff leadership and ultimately for compliance by a qualified board member. The chief executive should ensure that appropriate employees are trained and that they understand and accept internal fiscal controls.

The chief executive is responsible for hiring and managing staff with requisite experience and training to appropriately manage the financial functions of the organization.

The chief executive oversees and manages the internal process of completing the annual audit or independent cash review and institutes whatever changes are required by the board as a result of audit findings. The board leader or qualified financial professional should regularly review progress in addressing any requirements of the annual audit or financial review.

Additionally, important internal controls must be in place for fundraising. The chief executive should ensure compliance with all applicable local, state, and federal requirements in regard to fundraising activities. For example, registration is required in many states for certain fundraising activities. Since the rules vary from state to state, check with your state attorney general's office for current regulations. You must have policies that ensure restricted contributions are *never* compromised.

Often, donors, funders, underwriters, or others will restrict a gift or designate a specific use for the gift. Appropriate internal controls on these types of gifts will not allow them to be used for anything other than the donor's intended purpose. If that intent is betrayed, the donor or your state's attorney general could rescind the gift and even seek legal action against your nonprofit. Ultimately, it is the responsibility of the board to ensure these controls are adequate and in place, while the day-to-day management of fundraising is delegated to the chief executive to manage.

Many organizations institute an internal control requiring that any employee who handles cash or other donations must be bonded. While not a requirement, this is a sound fiscal practice you and your board should consider.

A chief executive learned the importance of having a crystal-clear gift-acceptance policy the hard way. A board member and her husband made a significant cash gift to the agency with a rather vague restriction on its use. The chief executive determined what she believed was an appropriate use of the donation. When the donors learned how their contribution was put to use, they disagreed strongly and demanded the gift be returned. Ultimately, this disagreement involved attorneys and lawsuits and was not settled to anyone's satisfaction. This situation could have avoided if the agency had clear gift-acceptance policies and these policies had been discussed with the donor in advance of the gift.

watch out!

Finally, the IRS Form 990 asks if the board has reviewed the document before it is filed, and that is certainly a good practice. After all, this is a public document, so it is important that all board members and leadership staff have reviewed the document in advance and that they are familiar and comply with the rules governing access to the document.

Review and Clarify the Invisible Yellow Line in Your Financial Management

This worksheet will help you clarify the Invisible Yellow Line in your organization's financial management. You might complete it individually and then share the results to start a conversation about how you will define the Invisible Yellow Line to operate most effectively and efficiently. Just open the lines of communication using this worksheet to avoid assumptions and confusion.

Discuss the key activity and decide for your organization who has primary responsibility at this time: board, board leader, chief executive, or other staff member. Or is it a shared responsibility?

The Invisible Yellow Line in Financial Management

Key Activity	Responsibility
Who has ultimate responsibility for fiscal and financial oversight?	
Who requires adequate accounting and financial reporting to support the organization's governance and management functions?	
Who ensures financial transparency to stakeholders and regulatory bodies?	
Who reviews the budget and regularly compares it with the actual figures?	
Who explains variances from budget over or under a specified amount?	
Who monitors day-to-day revenue and expenditures?	

Key Activity	Responsibility
Who performs an annual cost/benefit analysis of all programs and services?	
Who ensures the budget is realistic and adequate to achieve the long-term vision for the organization?	
Who participates in the annual budgeting process?	
Who reviews and sets staff salaries and benefits?	
Who sets the chief executive's salary and benefits?	
Who uses contemporaneous information to determine the CEO's salary and benefits?	
Who sets policies regarding the authority to sign contracts and documents for the organization?	
Who authorizes an annual audit or independent cash review?	
Who manages the audit or independent review process?	
Who reviews and accepts the annual audit or financial review and acts appropriately on recommendations?	
Who ensures that adequate financial reserves are in place?	
Who ensures that written fiscal policies and procedures are current and are followed consistently?	
Who develops an investment policy?	
Who ensures that a whistle-blower policy is in place?	
Who is responsible for ensuring that restricted funds are never used for purposes other than for the purposes the donor has designated?	
Who ensures that a gift-acceptance policy for tangible and intangible donations is in place?	
Who ensures that bank statements are reconciled by someone without signature authority?	
Who has appropriate qualifications to assess internal controls and provide regular financial statements to the board?	
Who ensures timely compliance with all local, state, and federal reporting requirements?	
Who ensures that internal controls for fundraising are current and compliant with all regulations?	

Key Activity	Responsibility
Who reviews the annual IRS Form 990 before it is filed?	
Who is responsible for ensuring that all employees who handle checks are cash bonded?	
Who follows the rules governing access to the IRS Form 990?	

To Recap

◆ The board has ultimate responsibility for financial oversight.

◆ The board has ultimate responsibility for adequate and appropriate fiscal planning, review, controls, and reporting.

◆ The chief executive and staff manage the day-to-day financial operations, develop internal controls, and regularly update internal policies and controls to ensure compliance with regulatory bodies.

Chapter Five

The Invisible Yellow Line in Planning

IN THIS CHAPTER

- ---→ Planning participants
- ---→ Planning that works
- ---→ Keeping the plan alive
- ---→ Leadership succession planning

Does the mere thought of a strategic planning session make your eyes roll back into your head or fill you with guilt and dread because you can't even remember where you filed the current plan?

It doesn't have to be that way! Well-run nonprofits welcome the opportunity to step back from their regular duties and plan for the future of the organization. This is so important that board and staff leaders should include the annual planning meeting in the calendar of events so that everyone can plan for this critical meeting in advance. The strategic planning session should result in action plans for the coming year that will focus the work of the board and staff and form the basis for goals for the board, its committees, the chief executive, and the organization's staff.

Who Participates in the Annual Planning Retreat?

The annual planning retreat is an opportunity to strengthen the partnership between board and senior staff. Both have valuable insights into the status and plans for your organization. Planning is not likely to succeed if key people aren't at the table. I believe there is a high value

Do your eyes roll back in your head at the mere thought of a strategic planning session?

in hearing from all perspectives and gaining "ownership" of the plan by all members of the board and senior staff.

Another benefit of including the full board and staff leaders in the planning process is that it will give both teams an opportunity to discuss and gain consensus on the ultimate goal of the game at hand—the sustainability of your organization.

Ultimately, effective planning is a result of both board and staff teams working together to achieve the same result, a plan of action for both the board and the staff to keep them focused on achieving strategic organizational goals.

The Board's Role in Strategic Planning

I strongly advocate that strategic planning is the role of the entire board, not just a select few. This process is far too important not to involve all those whose responsibility it is to lead a nonprofit organization. Some boards create a strategic planning committee to manage the planning process itself and to hold the board and the organization accountable for follow-up and completion of goals. In any case, the full board should participate in the planning process.

The Chief Executive's and Staff's Roles in Strategic Planning

The chief executive participates in strategic planning and decides which other key leadership staff should also be at the planning table. Again, I'd advocate that key staff leaders should participate in the planning process because they will bring a unique perspective of how plans will affect the organization's actual operations.

The Facilitator's Role in Strategic Planning

Should you include an independent facilitator? Likely, yes. A skilled facilitator can keep the group focused on outcomes and results, keep the business of the retreat moving, and present independent observations that can elevate the discussions to a more strategic level.

A nonprofit invested several thousand dollars and untold hours in a strategic planning process that took place over several months. When the plan was finally written by the facilitator, the organization's staff and board breathed a big sigh of relief and promptly filed the document away, patting themselves on the backs for having survived the arduous process. Too bad. All that money and time wasted. The facilitator, not the board and staff, wrote the plan, so the board and staff didn't "own it." And since the process took so long, no one wanted to even look at the plan again, and it merely gathered dust.

There are several ways to find an experienced facilitator. Ask other nonprofit stakeholders in your area who they recommend. Consider trading the responsibility with a skilled board leader or chief executive of another nonprofit. Perhaps there is expertise to be found at a nearby educational institution or corporation.

Interview the facilitator in advance, check references, and agree to outcomes and results you expect to achieve as a part of the planning process. Hold the facilitator accountable for achieving the results you require. It is important that the facilitator is a match for your organization's style. Some organizations need a facilitator merely to keep the planning meeting on target, while some organizations will require a deeper, longer involvement from the facilitator.

It is a good idea to begin the annual planning process with a meeting of board and staff leaders and the facilitator to agree on format, focus, and outcomes to be achieved so that everyone is on the same page.

What's Important to Include in a Planning Meeting?

I strongly recommend that you start each planning meeting with identifying a five-year (or longer) vision for your organization. The vision should be big, broad, and motivating. It probably states a perfect world where your organization has accomplished all it set out to do.

Then review the mission statement to ensure that it states who you are and how you will achieve the vision.

Review the previous year's strategic plan, celebrate accomplishments, and identify any outstanding issues.

Next, identify short-term priorities to address the vision. You can get your arms around a twelve- to eighteen-month list of three to five priorities, and this will keep board and staff focused on what needs to be accomplished.

What Comes Next? Board and Staff Committees and Action Plans

After the initial planning meeting is completed, board and staff should develop action plans, with key activities, accountability, and timelines for completion.

If your board is small, the whole board can participate in this process with key staff participants. If it is larger, the board leader, chief executive, or facilitator should assign breakout groups to develop the preliminary action plans and share them with the entire group.

Allow board members to identify their area(s) of passion or expertise so they may sign up to help execute follow-up tasks. Include senior staff in these planning groups since they will serve as the internal liaisons and will contribute valuable insights into resources in place or needed to achieve the plans.

Next steps and follow-up: The board leader endorses committees or task forces for each priority area, identifying a committee chair and members. The chief executive makes staff assignments to committees for support and follow-up.

It's a good idea to recruit nonboard members to these board committees to spread the work around and add valuable expertise. Be sure your bylaws don't prohibit this. If they do, consider amending them to allow nonboard members to serve on committees.

> Accountability and target dates for completion are critical to achieving planning goals.
>
> **principle**

Committees should meet within thirty days after the initial planning meeting to flesh out action plans. Committee chairs should then present action plans to the full board for review and acceptance. This will clarify overlap or identify stresses in internal or external resources.

It is the board and staff leader's responsibility to hold committees responsible for this important step in the process.

Easy Planning Format

Instead of an outline format that ends up as a list of "Things to Be Done," consider this simple planning format. Keep the key activities to no more than about ten to keep the initial focus on broad categories.

Goal or priority: _____

Key Activity	Responsibility	Target Date	Status

After broad categories of key activities are listed, assign ownership for each activity. Committees can then use the same format to break each large activity into smaller, bite-sized pieces with accountability and target dates.

This simple task list breaks big plans into smaller, bite-sized pieces. It provides a calendared to-do list with accountability for every step in the plan. This easy planning format can provide focus for board and staff for the short term and will lead to achievement of longer term visions.

The Board Leader and Chief Executive's Role in Keeping the Plan Alive

When the board leader and the chief executive develop the agenda for each board and staff meeting, you should include status reports on the plan's key activities to date. Review progress. Identify molehills before they become mountains. Adopt changes as required. *Anticipate* rather than react.

The chief executive and board leader can develop the CEO's annual goals to focus on activities to be achieved within the strategic plan and annual plan of work. Then the board can evaluate the CEO annually on the basis of achieving specific goals within the strategic plan and annual plan of work.

> If your entire organization from board to staff is focused on the priorities and goals set at a strategic planning meeting and the work of both board and staff is focused on action plans that follow the overall strategic plan, you will be amazed at how much can be accomplished by both sides of the Invisible Yellow Line with far less confusion and contention.
>
>  practical tip

The chief executive can also work with staff leadership to develop individual goals and departmental goals within the strategic plan and annual plan of work. Staff leaders can be evaluated annually for performance of specific goals within the strategic plan and annual plan of work, as they will evaluate their staff members, and so on.

Committee Reporting

Unfortunately, an enthusiastic committee chair can spend valuable board meeting time with details of the committee's work. Not only does this take up valuable time, but it also invites micromanaging of the committee by the full board.

I recommend adopting a format for committee reports that is submitted in writing with the board meeting materials in advance of the board meeting. That way, any questions may be addressed to the committee chair prior to the full board meeting to save valuable board meeting time. Since the full board will have seen the committee's work plan after the annual planning meeting, there may be no need for a verbal committee report at all!

Here is the format I use:

Committee: _____

Committee chair: _____

Date: _____

Ongoing actions within the strategic plan:

◆

◆

◆

◆

Issues requiring board discussion or action with documentation:

◆

◆

◆

Now that plans are in place that will focus on achievement of long-term visions and goals, let's discuss an often-overlooked issue: leadership succession planning.

A leadership succession plan answers the question "Who's up next?"

important

Board Leadership Succession Planning

Succession planning answers the question "Who comes next?" Does the end of the year bring uncomfortable questioning about who will take the lead for the coming year? Does board leadership fall on the shoulders of the same person(s) over and over? It shouldn't, nor should the chief executive insinuate the appointment of someone who can be controlled by the CEO.

Instead, your board's bylaws should provide for a logical progression to leadership, such as this: the board develops a three-year commitment for the board leader consisting of one year as leader-elect, one year as leader, and one year as past leader. The nominating committee (or other leadership committee) of the board should take a long-term view of the board's leadership and identify exceptional leaders who will step up to lead. Perhaps the emerging leader will need training in leadership skills. If the new leader's role is established in advance, training can easily be accomplished.

Certainly, the chief executive can play a role in the process to identify the new board leadership, but the role is an advisory role, not a voting role.

A good board leader has much to share about what works, what doesn't, and lessons learned. You can keep the past-leader involved as a mentor to the leader-elect and the current leader to take advantage of this knowledge and experience.

I am beginning to see some bylaws that require a two-year commitment for the board leader, and that's not a bad idea. As we discussed earlier, it isn't easy leading a nonprofit board, and two years in the leadership role might allow for a more productive term of office to accomplish longer-term objectives for the full board and the organization as a whole. You might even consider this model for key board leadership positions, including treasurer and secretary. This model might require an amendment to your bylaws, but it may be worthwhile to ensure the leadership succession plan.

> Why does a three-year leadership succession plan work? Leading the board is not an easy task. There is so much to be learned about governance, planning, financial management, and the basic how-tos of managing a board. Spending a year as the leader-elect allows for learning, training, and planning in a less demanding role. Then the year as leader can begin immediately with all the preliminaries out of the way. Let's face it; a year goes by quickly, and if much of it is spent getting organized, far too much time is wasted.
>
> **observation**

Review and Clarify the Invisible Yellow Line in Your Planning Process

This worksheet will help you clarify the Invisible Yellow Line in planning in your organization. You might complete it individually and then share the results to start a conversation about how you will define the Invisible Yellow Line to operate most effectively and efficiently. The Yellow Line is invisible. It moves. Each organization might define its position differently. The important thing to remember is that there are not always "right" answers. Just open the lines of communication using this worksheet to avoid assumptions and confusion.

Discuss the key activity and decide for your organization who has primary responsibility at this time: board, board leader, chief executive, or other staff member. Or is it a shared responsibility?

The Invisible Yellow Line in Planning

Key Activity	Responsibility
Who sets a specific date each year for strategic planning?	
Who participates in annual strategic planning?	
Who ensures that mission review is a part of annual strategic planning?	
Who develops five-year visions that provide the framework for short-term goals?	

Key Activity	Responsibility
Who appoints committees as required to complete the annual work plan?	
Who serves as liaison to board committees?	
Who ensures that the annual strategic plan focuses the work of board committees and staff?	
Who ensures that the plan of work includes key activities, accountability, and target dates?	
Who provides that board committees may include nonboard members?	
Who requires committees to develop action plans to achieve the strategic plan?	
Who sets the agenda for board meetings that include status reports on the strategic plan?	
Who requires committees to use written status reports?	
Who does not micromanage the committees?	
Who evaluates the CEO and staff leaders on achievement of goals within the annual plan of work?	
Who ensures that a leadership succession plan is in place, as required in the bylaws?	

To Recap

◆ The full board and leadership staff should participate in the planning process.

◆ Use the annual plan of work to focus board and staff on priorities.

◆ An effective strategic plan includes key activities, accountability, and target dates.

◆ Keep the plan alive with regular progress reports at board and staff meetings.

Chapter Six

The Invisible Yellow Line in Human Resources

IN THIS CHAPTER

- ---→ The board's primary roles in human resources

- ---→ The chief executive's primary roles in human resources

- ---→ Thoughts on the chief executive's report to the board

One of the most difficult and confusing issues in nonprofit management involves human resources, so it should be a critical discussion topic for organizational leaders on both sides of the Invisible Yellow Line.

The Board's Primary Role in Human Resources

The board hires, evaluates, manages, disciplines, and has authority to terminate the chief executive *only*. The board also develops the job description for the chief executive *only,* although key members of the board who have human resources expertise may be involved in general review of staff job descriptions. The board sets the compensation for the CEO. The board is not involved in hiring or setting compensation for any staff members other than the CEO. The board should use comparative data when setting the chief executive's compensation, as referred to in the current annual IRS Form 990. The board may approve the need for hiring additional staff, but it does not get involved in the hiring process.

It is a conventional practice for the board leader or executive committee to hold an annual performance evaluation of the chief executive. As we discussed in the previous chapter on planning, the board leader or executive committee should set the chief executive's annual plan of work within the framework of the organization's strategic plan. In some organizations, the board leader alone evaluates the chief executive. In others, the executive committee holds the annual evaluation. It is unwieldy (and pretty difficult to control) if the full board participates in the annual evaluation of the chief executive. Perhaps a better model is for the board leader to get input from those board members who wish to comment and then hold the actual evaluation alone or with the executive committee only.

> How often should the chief executive ask for a performance evaluation? Is once a year often enough to stay on track?
>
> **food for thought**

Personally, as a former chief executive, I requested this evaluation process quarterly so that there were no surprises at year-end and we could keep the lines of communication open, addressing problems before they became highly contested Yellow Line issues.

Board members do not get involved in the day-to-day management of staff—unless, of course, there is need to become involved due to a grievance or other legal issue. If there is a need to go beyond the chief executive, the board must carefully follow your organization's policies in regard to who reports, who investigates, and who on the board has authority to do so. Board members must follow the chain of command as defined in board and organizational policies.

Be sure that your organizational policies state the appropriate board leader or committee to receive complaints in a grievance or whistle-blower scenario and be sure to include review of these policies in new-board-member orientation. It's not a bad idea to hold refresher courses in these policies for the full board on occasion.

If your organization has a large staff, it is a good idea for the board to include a professional with human resources expertise to ensure that all human resources policies and procedures are current and compliant with regulations. If this professional is not a member of the board or the staff, then the board should authorize funding for regular reviews and updates by a human resources professional.

> A disgruntled staff person who was friendly with a board member constantly complained about her salary, the chief executive, working conditions, and more. Naturally, the board member wanted to be attentive to her friend, the staff person, and soon crossed way over the Invisible Yellow Line by involving other board members in the discussions. Both the disgruntled staff person and well-meaning board members had gone around the organization's policies and acted outside the chain of command. Board and staff must receive training on how to deal with these types of issues.
>
> **watch out!**

The Chief Executive's Primary Role in Human Resources

The chief executive hires, evaluates, disciplines, and terminates the organization's staff. The CEO ensures that staff members have the requisite experience and training for their individual positions.

It is also the chief executive's responsibility to ensure that all human resource policies and procedures are reviewed regularly, are compliant with state and federal regulations, are posted in appropriate places when relevant, and are kept in compliance with state and federal guidelines in the case of personnel files. Additionally, the CEO ensures that new employees are oriented in key organizational policies such as the grievance policy, whistle-blower policy, confidentiality policy, etc. And the CEO ensures the required policies and procedures are in place for background checks for staff and volunteers as appropriate for your organization's programs and services.

Staff, including the chief executive, should have job descriptions and annual goals set to advance the annual plan of work. The chief executive ensures there is an annual evaluation process for all levels of staff. The CEO may perform these evaluations directly or may delegate the performance evaluations to other leadership staff for those they supervise directly. Just as we discussed previously with annual goals and evaluation of the chief executive, if every staff person's annual goals are set within the framework of your organization's strategic plan, it will be much easier to clarify the Invisible Yellow Line within the staff structure. Yes, indeed, there is an Invisible Yellow Line within the staff too!

Finally, the chief executive should budget for and support professional education and development efforts for staff, including memberships in related professional organizations and other ongoing training and education.

The Chief Executive's Report to the Board

Now is the time to put some thought into the traditional chief executive's report to the board. I've been on both sides of this Yellow Line issue, as chief executive and as board leader. Of course, as chief executive, you want the board to appreciate that you are valuable, working hard, managing myriad day-to-day issues, earning your salary ten times over, etc., etc., etc. Therefore, it is tempting to put a high level of detail into that monthly report to the board. But this can be a trap. The more detailed the report, the easier it is for board members to micromanage and get involved in the chief executive's job.

This problem can be avoided. The CEO can meet with the board leader at the beginning of the year and openly discuss channels of communication and the level of detail *required* to support the board's governance and fiduciary responsibilities. You can

A relatively new chief executive wanted to prove his value to the board that hired him, so he created a detailed executive director's report for every board meeting. In fact, it developed into a three- to four-page report each month. Within a few months, the CEO was complaining to me that the board was micromanaging him and the day-to-day operations of the organization. He then realized how he had invited this micromanagement by giving the board way too much detail. He had, in essence, invited the board to cross over the Invisible Yellow Line.

 stories from the real world

develop a format for the chief executive's report to demonstrate executive and staff progress within the goals and objectives of the strategic plan and annual plan of work. Keep the day-to-day details out of this monthly report.

Review and Clarify the Invisible Yellow Line in Human Resources

This worksheet will help you clarify the Invisible Yellow Line in human resources and then share the results to start a conversation about how you will define the Invisible Yellow Line to operate most effectively and efficiently. The Yellow Line is invisible. It moves. Each organization might define its position differently. The important thing to remember is that there are not always "right" answers. Just open the lines of communication using this worksheet to avoid assumptions and confusion.

Discuss the key activity and decide for your organization who has primary responsibility at this time: board, board leader, chief executive, or other staff member. Or is it a shared responsibility?

The Invisible Yellow Line in Human Resources

Key Activity	Responsibility
Who hires and supervises the chief executive?	
Who reports directly to the board?	
Who evaluates the chief executive annually?	
Who sets the compensation for the chief executive?	
Who does not review compensation for individual staff members other than the chief executive?	
Who uses comparative data in setting the chief executive's compensation?	
Whose annual goals and objectives are approved by the executive committee or full board?	
Who may approve the need to hire additional staff but does not participate in the hiring process?	
Who respects the chain of command and does not get involved in staff issues, disputes, or other issues falling outside established policies?	
Who receives training on the organization's grievance and whistle-blower policies?	
Who provides necessary oversight to ensure human resource policies are followed?	
Who ensures that human resource policies are current and compliant with all regulations?	

Key Activity	Responsibility
Who is responsible for day-to-day management of staff?	
Who hires and supervises staff?	
Who performs or directs annual staff performance evaluations based on agreed-upon goals and objectives within the strategic plan and annual plan of work?	
Who handles staff complaints through the chain of command?	
Who ensures that appropriate background and security checks are in place for staff and volunteers?	
Who reviews and updates job descriptions for all paid staff positions?	
Who reviews personnel policies annually for compliance with local, state, and federal requirements?	
Who supports professional development training and professional memberships for staff?	
Who ensures that employees are trained in personnel policies, that they've received a copy of the policies, and that they've signed a document stating their acceptance of the policies?	

To Recap

◆ The board and chief executive manage human resources for the organization, but on different planes.

◆ Both staff and board have key responsibilities in the areas of human resources policies and procedures.

◆ The board manages only the chief executive.

◆ The chief executive is responsible for staff management.

Chapter Seven

The Invisible Yellow Line in Resource Development

IN THIS CHAPTER

---→ The board's role in resource development

---→ The staff's role in resource development

---→ Resource development planning

Question: Whose responsibility is it for ensuring adequate financial resources to sustain a nonprofit organization? You know the answer. This responsibility belongs to both the board and the staff teams. They may play different roles, but both sides of the Yellow Line have equally important resource development responsibilities. Board members give and get. Staff members support board members in giving and getting, ensuring that appropriate internal fundraising policies and procedures are in place and keeping track of the day-to-day resource development activities.

While the development plan is usually created by the staff, it is the board's responsibility to ensure that revenue projections are realistic and attainable. The board should regularly review revenue results within the development plan, reacting to shortfalls and requiring a plan to ensure that critical programs, services, and staff are not compromised. Without effective resource development, your mission is at risk, so both teams have to work together and meet in the middle.

Board Resource Development Committees

Many boards create a resource development committee that provides the initial oversight of all fundraising and resource development efforts. This is the committee that works with staff to create and present the annual development plan to the full board for acceptance. The

> Whose responsibility is it to develop the financial resources required to operate effectively and efficiently? You know the answer!
>
> **principle**

resource development committee also sets the example for the rest of the board in giving and getting and in support of your organization's development efforts. This committee regularly reviews the staff's evaluation of resource development efforts.

Another key board committee is a planned giving advisory committee. There are four professional advisors who should be on this committee: a wills/estate/tax attorney, a CPA, a financial planner, and an insurance broker. Ask them to provide basic training to the board and to your supporters through the organization's website, in newsletters, and through other vehicles to educate your stakeholders on how they can take advantage of the various planned giving avenues.

The Board's Role in Giving

Board members should actively support fundraising events and activities. Board members should provide oversight by evaluating the actual results of fundraising activities. Board members should act strategically to anticipate fundraising shortfalls and ensure there are plans in place to protect vital organizational resources.

Your board should attain 100 percent board giving every year. You will find that more and more grantors and donors are asking, "What percentage of your board makes an annual gift to support your organization? Why should I give if they don't?" This is often a requirement of many granting organizations. Therefore, to ensure your organization has the financial resources required to meet its mission and purpose, board members should set the example for other organizational stakeholders by making annual financial contributions.

> Does every board member have to make an annual financial gift? Yes. Does everyone have to give the same amount? No. But every member of the board should give what is *personally meaningful* every year. Leave nothing to chance—include this requirement in your board member job description.
>
> **principle**

There are organizations that have established a set amount or minimum amount for every board member. Although this certainly levels the playing field, it might limit your board's diversity of time, talent, and treasure.

Oh, by the way, ensuring 100 percent annual giving is the board leader's responsibility and *not* the chief executive's. Board members report to the board leader. The board leader should follow up individually with any member who does not commit, or does not fulfill that commitment, so that the integrity of the full board's 100 percent commitment is not compromised.

The Board's Role in Getting

Board members should be active in both giving and getting the financial and in-kind resources necessary to sustain the organization they lead. Consider this: the value of the power, influence, and reach of one or two staff members versus the power, influence, and reach of dozens of board volunteers. Certainly, the more people asking and reaching out, the more you will get.

> The board leaders should guarantee to stakeholders that the board has set the example for financial support by achieving 100 percent board giving every year at a personally meaningful level for each board member.
>
> **principle**

Board members should attend and participate actively in your organization's important fundraising events as an example of their support. They should buy their tickets and make their contributions first.

Money isn't the only thing that board members can get for your organization. Consider the important impact in-kind contributions, both tangible and intangible, can have on reducing expenses. Encourage board members who might be shy about asking for financial support to consider how they can leverage their sphere of influence to recruit in-kind contributions.

How to Make Giving and Getting Work for the Board

Start at the beginning with no surprises. A board job description can make it abundantly clear that all board members are expected to give and get. It's not fair to skip over this important requirement and hope a board volunteer will just "get it." It's not fair to the board volunteer, and it's not fair to your organization. A sample board job description is included in **Appendix C**.

You can provide fundraising training and suggest ways for board members to get involved in giving and getting that will be satisfying and successful. Celebrate their successes.

There are many ways a board member can support resource development other than bringing a list of twenty people they will ask for money. (Board members really dread and resist this conversation.) Some fundraising ideas for your board are included in **Appendix B**.

The Board's Role in Thanking and Acknowledging

Here are some important questions: Does your board know who the organization's top givers are? Does the board get involved in thanking and recognizing these top donors? What if a top giver knows a board member personally or professionally and does not receive a personal thank-you? Don't let these embarrassing events happen to your board. Instead, give the board regular opportunities to review names of the top givers and commit to calling, writing, or visiting (in the case of a major gift) to say thank you.

The Staff's Role in Resource Development

The chief executive officer and staff have primary responsibility for the day-to-day management and administration of all resource development efforts and should support the board in its development efforts. In many organizations, much of the day-to-day resource development responsibility is delegated to a development officer with formal oversight by the chief executive.

> An organization received a significant donation at year-end. Later that month, a board member sat next to the donor at a community meeting. The donor was expecting the board member to acknowledge his donation, but no acknowledgment was made. Why? The board member simply wasn't aware of the donation. The result? The donor felt unappreciated and that the organization didn't recognize the value of his large gift. I wonder how many times this has happened in your organization?
>
>  **stories from the real world**

The staff should prepare the annual resource development plan for the board's acceptance.

Staff should keep the board informed and involved in resource development efforts by presenting regular updates to the board about the results and outcomes of the resource development plan.

If an unanticipated loss or reduction in revenue occurs, the chief executive should present options to the board to replace the lost revenue to protect your valuable organizational programs and services.

Additionally, the staff has responsibility for fundraising via your organization's website, providing a secure method of donating online, recognizing donors appropriately, updating messages that encourage and reward giving, and showing the results of investment in your organization.

Oversight, Regulations, Policies, and Compliance

The chief executive and key development staff also carry the internal day-to-day responsibility of understanding and complying with the numerous federal oversight guidelines and regulations that apply to your organization's resource development programs. It is critical that as staff, you know, understand, and stay current with these regulations.

The IRS has several rules and regulations regarding how your organization thanks and acknowledges donations, how it defines unrelated business income for tax purposes, what it defines as advertising revenue, how to handle and record sponsorships, and more. It is a good idea to stay current with IRS publications such as Publication 598 and Publication 1771.

> Although compliance with rules and regulations can be considered primarily to rest on the staff side of the Invisible Yellow Line, let us repeat here that the board has the ultimate responsibility for ensuring that regulations are understood and followed.
>
> **observation**

Recently, states have started paying considerable attention to fundraising and the use of fundraising consultants or fundraising programs via the Internet. Many states require that fundraising consultants and Internet providers, and nonprofits in most cases, be registered and pay a fee. Be sure you are in compliance.

While we'd like to think that a nonprofit is immune to embezzlement or fraud, the potential for fraud is a fact of life in all organizations. It is critical that your internal controls provide oversight and clear guidelines for how contributions are received, receipted, and recorded.

We discussed in a previous chapter the importance of understanding and following federal regulations in regard to fiscal controls. These controls also play a part in your donor relations program, especially in receipting and acknowledging sponsorships and underwriting. Be sure you understand and comply with IRS Publication 598, which describes unrelated business income tax (UBIT). How you give a sponsor benefits in return for sponsorship might mean the sponsorship should be considered as unrelated business income.

Donor Relations

The staff has primary responsibility for ensuring that exceptional donor relations are a high priority even though your board can have a positive impact in thanking, as we discussed previously in this chapter.

The IRS has guidelines you should follow in thanking and acknowledging donors for contributions. Today, a donor must have acknowledgment from a nonprofit for any single cash contribution of more than $250 annually. Don't wait for the donor to ask. Instead, be sure your donor relations program includes ways to initiate the acknowledgment quickly by year-end. Or, better yet, institute a policy of thanking every time a gift is received, with the total acknowledged at year-end.

Some donors want to be publicly recognized for their contributions, and it is important to do so. Others, however, prefer to remain anonymous. It is important that your donor relations procedures respond correctly, especially if you involve the board in thanking donors.

Internal policies and procedures must be in place to ensure that restricted gifts (both tangible and intangible) are never compromised and that the donor's intent is followed to the letter.

Staff is also responsible for creating and maintaining a donor database that is current and allows for excellent donor relations.

Review and Clarify the Invisible Yellow Line in Resource Development

This worksheet will help you clarify the Invisible Yellow Line in resource development in your organization. You might complete it individually and then share the results to start a conversation about how you will define the Invisible Yellow Line to operate most effectively and efficiently. The Yellow Line is invisible. It moves. Each organization might define its position differently. The important thing to remember is that there are not always "right" answers. Just open the lines of communication using this worksheet to avoid assumptions and confusion.

Discuss the key activity and decide for your organization who has primary responsibility at this time: board, board leader, chief executive, or other staff member. Or is it a shared responsibility?

The Invisible Yellow Line in Resource Development

Key Activity	Responsibility
Who has an active resource development committee?	
Who should make meaningful personal financial contributions every year?	
Who leverages their spheres of influence to support your fundraising efforts?	
Who ensures 100 percent annual giving?	
Who appoints a planned giving committee or a subcommittee to address planned giving?	
Who anticipates reductions in funding in advance and ensures that plans are in place to reduce expenses or increase revenue?	
Who evaluates the cost/benefit of all fundraising activities annually?	
Whose job description includes the annual giving requirement?	
Who attends and supports fundraising events?	
Who participates in thanking the top level of givers?	
Who finds and solicits in-kind contributions and services to reduce annual expenses?	
Who ensures that recruitment and orientation includes fundraising expectations and training for board members?	
Who writes the development plan that contains diverse revenue elements?	
Who reviews all fundraising efforts annually to ensure their effective use of resources and return on investment?	
Who ensures that sponsor acknowledgments do not initiate UBIT?	

Key Activity	Responsibility
Who is responsible for ensuring that Internet fundraising is in compliance with state regulations for registration?	
Who ensures that fraud-prevention procedures regarding handling of donations are in place?	
Who is responsible for ensuring that all fundraising efforts are in compliance with local, state, and federal regulations?	
Who ensures compliance with IRS guidelines for UBIT, evaluation of gifts, acknowledgments, etc.?	
Who is responsible for ensuring that restricted donations are never compromised?	
Who sends acknowledgments for contributions in a timely fashion in compliance with IRS regulations?	
Who makes quick turnaround a high priority for donor thanking and acknowledgments?	
Who is responsible for ensuring the website has effective methods for promoting and receiving online contributions in a secure manner?	

To Recap

◆ The board provides oversight for the organization's resource development programs, and the staff takes responsibility for day-to-day operation and management of fundraising programs.

◆ The board sets the example for others by achieving 100 percent annual giving.

◆ The organization reviews and evaluates the effectiveness of resource development efforts, anticipating and planning for shortfalls to protect programs and services.

Chapter Eight

The Invisible Yellow Line in Board Recruitment

IN THIS CHAPTER

···→ Board and staff roles in the recruitment process

···→ The role of the nominating committee

···→ Board and staff roles in the nominating committee

It's the month or two before the annual meeting, and the chief executive officer nudges the board chair as a reminder that terms are expiring and new members must be recruited to fill the empty seats on the board. Confusion results as board members, including the board leader, ask the chief executive to confirm the status of their terms. Then, after determining that five new members should be recruited, the board chair asks, "Does anyone know anybody good who can serve on this board?"

Does this sound familiar?

Or here's another situation. Tradition in an organization requires that board members find their replacements when their terms expire or they resign.

Or another situation. The chief executive takes the primary responsibility for recruiting new board members—in essence, hiring that CEO's own bosses. This is far too often the case when a founder has transitioned into the chief executive position and has not clarified the Yellow Line between board and staff roles, trying to take on both.

None of these approaches will create and build a board of the right people who have the right skills to effectively govern your nonprofit organization.

Instead, let's look at a different model: using a nominating committee that works year-round to find and fill the open board seats with a balance of skills and expertise required to lead your organization appropriately.

Creating an Effective Nominating Committee

Your nominating committee can actively seek *new* board members with *new* ideas, *new* contacts, *different* experiences, or it can merely re-create the current board. While the latter might be easier to manage, you must ask yourself how your organization will meet challenges by maintaining the status quo. Rather, I think you want board members who challenge the status quo and suggest new ways of doing and thinking.

> Think of the importance of the nominating committee this way: the nominating committee is responsible for the future of your organization. If the right people are on the board, your organization can thrive. If not . . .
>
> **food for thought**

The nominating committee might just be the most important committee of your board of directors. It ought to be a standing committee in your bylaws so its importance is never neglected.

Ultimately, it is the responsibility of the board to recruit board volunteers whose skills, experience, and expertise will lead the organization and ensure that it serves its mission and purpose.

The chief executive should be a nonvoting member of the nominating committee to prevent conflicts of interest and confusion as to roles. (The chief executive is employed *by* the board and reports *to* the board.) The CEO's major role in the recruitment process lies in helping the board identify the skills required to govern and manage effectively.

There are other key players in your board nominating process. If the only people serving on the nominating committee are board members, you've narrowed your scope. Instead, consider asking community leaders, people with connections to the skills you need, and others with "reach" to join the nominating committee as advisory or ex officio members.

Who Should Chair This Critical Committee?

There are three models that work best:

◆ The leader-elect of the board can chair the nominating committee. After all, who has a more vested interest in ensuring that a strong board is in place?

◆ The immediate past-leader of the board can chair the nominating committee. This important role reinforces the value of the past leader and keeps this person involved.

◆ A seasoned member of the board who knows and understands the vital role of recruiting the best candidates for the board can chair the nominating committee.

The Recruitment Process

Rather than looking for people who mirror the current board, just building a list of names, or leaving this critical job to the chief executive, start by identifying what *skills* are required to govern your organization and move it forward.

> What *doesn't work* is placing the critically important role of chairing the nominating committee on the shoulders of Good Old Bob, who's been on the board forever and is someone you don't know what to do with! I warn you that GOB will merely recruit more like himself, and that is a recipe for sameness and stagnation.
>
> What also *doesn't work* is allowing the chief executive to hand-pick board members who won't cause conflict with the CEO's leadership and management or to select players who won't challenge the chief executive in any way. This really shifts the Yellow Line out of alignment!
>
> **watch out!**

Create a Matrix

Include both the board and the chief executive in this process. Keep it simple—a table format with five or six columns will do.

Identify those *skills* required to achieve your goals, serve your mission, and provide a diversity of experience. List these skills in the first column of your matrix.

> Develop a matrix of *what skills* are required to best serve your organization's mission, then brainstorm about when you need that skill and *who* might best bring that critical skill.
>
>  practical tip

Typically, you will want skills such as legal, financial, public relations/marketing, fundraising, human resources, advocacy, and the like. But you may need client or consumer representation, site or physical plant expertise, programming, and other skills that are dictated by your particular mission and purpose. Underlying all these skills, of course, is a passion and commitment to the mission. The chief executive plays an important role in this process, helping to identify the skills required to support the organization's operations.

For many organizations, it is also important to achieve diversity in age, gender, geography, and ethnicity. Others require consumer or client representation. Still others may require that the board have percentages of diversity represented. All these are critical to success (and even legality), so be sure your recruitment process is in line with your bylaw requirements.

A Typical Matrix

Skills We Need	When We Need Someone with these Skills	Potential Candidate	Is Candidate Connected to Our Organization? How?	Our Plan to Recruit Prospective Board Member

Once your team has agreed on the first column of required skills, indicate *when* you need to fill that slot. The idea here is to fill the skill slot before the current board member's term expires so that you have a better balance of expertise at all times. Of course, this isn't always possible, but it's worth striving for.

Now it is time to invite the ex officio members of the nominating committee to brainstorm with you about potential candidates for the board. You can involve these ex officio members in the recruiting process to make introductions if required.

A Variation on this Theme

If you lead a membership organization or association, your field of potential board candidates is probably narrowed somewhat by a requirement of membership. This should not pose a problem. Consider advisory nominating committee members from all sectors of your membership to ensure a more effective brainstorming session for potential candidates. Post requirements for board membership on your website to attract candidates and inform them of your expectations.

> If you start the nominating process a year in advance (the absolute best practice), you can invite a potential candidate to serve on a board committee that lends itself to the candidate's expertise. It's like dating. You each get the opportunity to size each other up and see if it's a fit.
>
> **observation**

Consistency is the Key to Effective Recruitment

I can tell you from years of experience that the wheels always fall off the board bus when new board members join and bring differing individual expectations about their service on the board.

> Inconsistency and confusion about board members' roles and expectations can cause the wheels to fall off the board bus.
>
> **principle**

Here's an example of what can happen. Board member Jane recruits her friend Mary and explains "all about serving on this great board." Board member John recruits a community leader and explains, "It takes just a few hours a year to serve." The chief executive recruits Andy and tells him he really doesn't need to attend many meetings . . . You see the trend here, I am sure.

Widely diverse messages about board service are the result of several different recruiters with different messages and opinions about what is expected of board members.

In this example, when the discussion of attendance, meetings, contributions, fundraising, and governance comes up, is it any wonder there could be a strong feeling from these newly recruited board members that the organization is disorganized and unprofessional and that they as new members have been hornswoggled? (I love that word and tried very hard to find a place for it in this book!)

Here's how to prevent this from happening.

The Chief Executive's Role in Recruitment

The chief executive can support an effective nominating process by creating a board recruitment packet that includes at least the following:

◆ Fact sheet about your organization (mission, vision, statistics, history, etc.)

◆ Financial information (budget, recent financial statement, etc.)

◆ Board job description (see **Appendix C** for a sample)

◆ Application for board membership (see **Appendix D** for a sample)

◆ Board annual commitment letter (see **Appendix F** for a sample)

◆ Code of ethics (your value system and how you operate)

◆ Board roster and organization chart (including business affiliation, board office held, term, etc.)

◆ Staff organization chart (how your organization is organized)

◆ D&O insurance statement

◆ Reimbursement policies (if any)

◆ Board orientation schedule

◆ Anything else that is important for a candidate to know in order to make an informed decision about whether or not to join your board

The Board's Role in Recruitment

Members of the board's nominating committee share this packet of information with a prospective board candidate, clearly identifying the expectations of time, talent (skill), and treasure (annual financial commitment) for each board member. If the prospective board member is not ready to serve on the board or you don't feel this person is a good match, you could invite the candidate to serve as an advisory member on a board committee.

The chief executive can certainly attend meetings with prospective board members to answer specific questions about the organization and present the staff's viewpoint.

The nominating committee presents the list of potential candidates to the full board or the organization's membership with the candidate's application for membership, referrals, or other pertinent information.

Once again, this might require a bylaws revision if this is not the process as currently defined. Although revising bylaws is not always easy, it's worth considering to improve your nominating process.

Review and Clarify the Invisible Yellow Line in Your Board Recruitment Process

This worksheet will help you clarify the Invisible Yellow Line in board recruitment in your organization. You might complete it individually and then share the results to start a conversation about how you will define the Invisible Yellow Line to operate most effectively and efficiently. The Yellow Line is invisible. It moves. Each organization might define its position differently. The important thing to remember is that there are not always "right" answers. Just open the lines of communication using this worksheet to avoid assumptions and confusion.

Discuss the key activity and decide for your organization who has primary responsibility at this time: board, board leader, chief executive, or other staff member. Or is it a shared responsibility?

The Invisible Yellow Line in Board Recruitment

Key Activity	Responsibility
Who is responsible for appointing a nominating committee as defined in the bylaws?	
Who is an ex officio, nonvoting member of the board nominating committee?	
Who appoints the leader of the nominating committee?	
Who appoints advisory members to the nominating committee?	
Who ensures that the board reflects the diversity, ethnicity, educational, and economic status required to serve our mission?	
Who develops a matrix of skills required to ensure exceptional board development?	
Who develops a recruitment packet to support the nominating process?	
Who requires an application for board membership?	
Who is an advisory member in the recruitment process?	
Who encourages potential members to serve on committees?	

To Recap

◆ An effective recruitment process will ensure that you find and get the right people on the board.

◆ Both the board and the chief executive actively participate in the recruitment process for board members, but the board takes the lead in recruitment of new board members.

◆ An effective nominating committee develops a matrix that identifies the skills required to serve your mission.

◆ Ensure that consistent messages are given to all prospective board members about your expectations of time, talent, and treasure.

Chapter Nine

Take the Invisible Yellow Line Test

IN THIS CHAPTER

---→ The Yellow Line test in governance, fiscal oversight, management, planning, human resources, resource development, and board recruitment

---→ How to use this test

---→ Final thoughts

Finally, I offer this test as a great way to open an annual discussion between board and staff leadership as to who does what, how they do it, and how leadership can best support each other. As suggested earlier, each organization is different and different circumstances will require different definitions and descriptions of the Invisible Yellow Line.

You can use this simple test to open lines of communication between board members and staff. Remember that there often is more than one "right" answer and that the answers may change as circumstances change. The point of the test is to get all parties to communicate, clarify roles, and agree about how your organization will manage these areas of responsibility, especially when there is a difference of opinion between board and staff.

Q: **Who appoints board committees?**

a. The board leader

b. The chief executive

c. The development officer

d. The past board leader

Q: Who supports the work of board committees?

   a. Hired contractors

   b. No one—they do it all themselves

   c. Designated staff liaisons

   d. Helpful volunteers

> Caution: the Invisible Yellow Line is *invisible*, so it is critical that board and staff leaders clarify *in advance* how you will deal with defining the Yellow Line in crucial organizational management areas.
>
>

Q: Who develops the board meeting agendas?

   a. Anyone can do it

   b. The board leader and chief executive

   c. The nominating committee chair

   d. A member of the administrative staff

Q: Who recruits new board members?

   a. Outgoing board members replace themselves

   b. We run an ad in the newspaper and interview respondents

   c. The nominating committee

   d. The chief executive

Q: Who assumes ultimate fiduciary responsibility for actions of the organization?

   a. The chief executive

   b. The organization's CFO

   c. The auditor

   d. The board of directors

Q: Who implements board and committee decisions?

   a. Hired contractors

   b. Board volunteers and staff liaisons

   c. Clients

   d. The board leader

Q: Who calendars and confirms an annual planning retreat?

   a. The retreat facilitator

   b. The board leader and chief executive

   c. The nominating committee chair

   d. The executive committee

Q: **Who approves major agency repair and upkeep expenses?**

    a. The janitor and maintenance person

    b. The chief executive

    c. A board committee

    d. The board leader

    e. The full board

Q: **Who approves major capital expenditures?**

    a. The funder who underwrites the capital campaign

    b. The building and grounds committee

    c. The chief executive

    d. The board leader

    e. The full board

Q: **Who prepares the preliminary budget?**

    a. The chief executive

    b. The organization's senior staff

    c. The budget and finance committee

    d. The executive committee

Q: **Who finalizes and approves the budget?**

    a. The chief executive

    b. The full board

    c. The organization's primary funder

    d. The organization's membership

Q: **Who monitors expenditures on a day-to-day basis?**

    a. Funding sources and donors

    b. The organization's CFO

    c. The executive committee

    d. The organization's senior staff

Q: **Who reviews the IRS Form 990 before it is filed?**

    a. The full board

    b. The auditor

    c. The organization's CFO

    d. The chief executive

Q: **Who ensures an annual independent audit or cash review is undertaken?**

   a. The organization's CFO

   b. The executive committee

   c. The chief executive

   d. The auditor

Q: **Who directs the planning process?**

   a. The chief executive

   b. The board leader

   c. The independent facilitator

   d. Volunteers

Q: **Who participates in the annual planning retreat?**

   a. Clients and volunteers

   b. Major donors

   c. Senior staff

   d. The full board of directors

Q: **Who provides input for the strategic plan?**

   a. Donors and funders

   b. Clients

   c. Senior staff

   d. The full board of directors

Q: **Who monitors achievement of goals?**

   a. Board committees and task forces

   b. The board leader

   c. The chief executive

   d. Donors and funders

Q: **Who approves the annual plan?**

   a. Senior staff

   b. The chief executive

   c. The board leader

   d. The full board of directors

Q: **Who hires and manages the chief executive?**

    a. The organization's human resources department

    b. The board leader

    c. The chief executive, without oversight

    d. The executive committee

Q: **Who directs the work of the staff?**

    a. The board of directors

    b. A board committee

    c. The chief executive and senior staff

    d. The board leader

Q: **Who evaluates staff performance?**

    a. The full board of directors

    b. The chief executive

    c. The board's human resources committee

    d. The board's committee chairs

Q: **Who evaluates the chief executive?**

    a. The board leader

    b. The board as a whole

    c. The executive committee

    d. Volunteers and donors

Q: **Who settles day-to-day problems among staff?**

    a. A board committee

    b. The chief executive and senior staff

    c. The board leader

    d. The executive committee

Q: **Who sets salaries for staff?**

    a. The full board of directors

    b. A board committee

    c. The chief executive

    d. The board leader

Q: Who reviews and approves personnel policies?

    a. A board committee

    b. An independent contractor

    c. The chief executive

    d. The full board

Q: Who promotes the organization within their personal sphere of influence?

    a. Anyone and everyone in the organization

    b. Only the chief executive

    c. A board committee

    d. Only the board leader

Q: Who recruits new board members?

    a. Outgoing board members (they find their own replacements)

    b. The chief executive

    c. The nominating committee

Q: Who chairs the board nominating committee?

    a. The chief executive

    b. An ex officio board member

    c. The board leader-elect, the past board leader, or a seasoned member of the board

    d. Good Old Bob

Q: Who appoints the nominating committee?

    a. The chief executive

    b. The board leader

Q: Who sets the example for stakeholders by making an annual financial contribution?

    a. Every member of the staff

    b. Every member of the board

    c. Both a. and b. above

Q: Who follows up and ensures 100 percent board giving?

    a. The chief executive

    b. The staff development officer

    c. The board leader

    d. No one

Q: **Who develops the initial resource development plan?**

    a. The board leader

    b. Major funders

    c. The CEO and staff

Q: **Who reviews the viability of all fundraising elements annually?**

    a. The board's resource development committee

    b. The full board

    c. The chief executive and staff

Q: **Who ensures that all fundraising programs comply with regulations?**

    a. The board leader

    b. The chief executive

    c. Staff members

How did you do on the test? The answers appear in **Appendix A**.

Final Thoughts

This manual was written to share my forty-five-plus years of experience in the nonprofit sector. I hope it has inspired you with easy, practical ideas that you can put to work quickly to clarify the Invisible Yellow Line in critical nonprofit management areas. You mission demands the best of both teams!

Thank you for your dedication and commitment to make this world a better place to live, work, and raise our families.

Appendix A

Answers to the Invisible Yellow Line Test

Remember, this tests the *Invisible Yellow Line*, so often there isn't a clear-cut right answer, and often there is more than one appropriate answer. The purpose of this test is to bring up the subjects and open lines of communication to avoid assumptions and conflict. I hope the simple test and the previous evaluation tables created some good conversations about the Invisible Yellow Line that will help clarify the primary board and staff roles in your organization's critical management categories.

Q: **Who appoints board committees?**

A: The board leader

Q: **Who supports the work of board committees?**

A: Designated staff liaisons

Q: **Who develops the board meeting agendas?**

A: The board leader and chief executive

Q: **Who recruits new board members?**

A: The nominating committee

Q: **Who assumes ultimate fiduciary responsibility for actions of the organization?**

A: The board of directors

Q: **Who implements board and committee decisions?**

A: Board volunteers and staff liaisons

Q: **Who calendars and confirms an annual planning retreat?**

A: The board leader and chief executive

Q: **Who approves major agency repair and upkeep expenses?**

A: A board committee, and/or the board leader, or the full board

Note: decisions on major expenditures might be delegated by the board to a committee, such as the executive committee, or to the board leader alone, but the full board often takes on this responsibility.

Q: **Who approves major capital expenditures?**

A: A board committee, and/or the board leader, or the full board

Note: decisions on major expenditures might be delegated by the board to a committee, such as the executive committee, or to the board leader alone but often, the full board takes on this responsibility.

Q: **Who prepares the preliminary budget?**

A: The chief executive, and/or the organization's senior staff, and/or the budget and finance committee, and/or the executive committee

Note: any or all of the answers are correct for the preliminary budget, but the board has ultimate authority for approval and acceptance.

Q: **Who finalizes and approves the budget?**

A: The full board or, in some cases, the organization's membership

Q: **Who monitors expenditures on a day-to-day basis?**

A: The organization's CFO and/or the organization's senior staff

Q: **Who reviews the IRS Form 990 before it is filed?**

A: The full board, the organization's CFO, and the chief executive

Q: **Who ensures an annual independent audit or cash review is undertaken?**

A: The executive committee and the chief executive

Q: **Who directs the planning process?**

A: The chief executive and the board leader

Q: **Who participates in the annual planning retreat?**

A: Senior staff and the full board of directors

Q: **Who provides input for the strategic plan?**

A: Senior staff and the full board of directors

Q: Who monitors achievement of goals?

A: The board leader (for board accomplishment) and the chief executive (for staff accomplishment)

Q: Who approves the annual plan?

A: The full board of directors

Q: Who hires and manages the chief executive?

A: The board leader or the executive committee

Q: Who directs the work of the staff?

A: The chief executive and senior staff

Q: Who evaluates staff performance?

A: The chief executive and senior staff

Q: Who evaluates the chief executive?

A: The board leader, and/or the board as a whole, and/or the executive committee

Note: any of the answers will work, but I do not advocate a full-board in-person evaluation.

Q: Who settles day-to-day problems among staff?

A: The chief executive and senior staff

Q: Who sets salaries for staff?

A: The chief executive and senior staff

Q: Who reviews and approves personnel policies?

A: A board committee, and/or the chief executive, and/or the full board

Note: all answers are correct at different phases of personnel policy creation, review, and implementation.

Q: Who promotes the organization within their personal sphere of influence?

A: Anyone and everyone in the organization

Q: Who recruits new board members?

A: The nominating committee

Q: Who chairs the board nominating committee?

A: The board leader-elect, the past board leader, or a seasoned member of the board

Q: **Who appoints the nominating committee?**

A: The board leader

Q: **Who sets the example for stakeholders by making an annual financial contribution?**

A: Every member of the board

Note: this should be a board requirement, but many staff members want to donate and should be given the opportunity to do so (but not as a requirement of employment).

Q: **Who follows up and ensures 100 percent board giving?**

A: The board leader

Q: **Who develops the initial resource development plan?**

A: The chief executive and staff

Q: **Who reviews the viability of all fundraising elements annually?**

A: The board's resource development committee, the full board, and the chief executive and staff

Note: the board leader and board have ultimate responsibility.

Q: **Who ensures all fundraising programs comply with regulations?**

A: The board leader, the chief executive, and staff members

Note: the board leader and board have ultimate responsibility.

Appendix B

Resource Development Activities Your Board Can Do Successfully

Ever wonder why there isn't a quorum at the board meeting when you ask board members to bring a list of twenty people they will ask for money this year? And, if there *is* a quorum, why most will have forgotten to bring the list—every month?

It's no wonder! Most board members don't relish the thought of asking their contacts for money, so here are some easy ways the board can get involved in fundraising that are painless *and* profitable!

Staff members can support the board in these fundraising endeavors by providing ideas, collateral materials, encouragement, and recognition of successful efforts.

1. **How board members can help with grants from foundations and corporations:**

   ◆ Research your own company's giving programs. Learn who makes the decisions, when decisions are made, what the company will fund (or not fund), how much to ask for, whether there is a specific process to be followed, and if there is a matching gift program.

   ◆ Research other companies' giving programs to learn the same as above.

   ◆ Provide testimonials, sign cover letters, or make corporate introductions to staff. The letter that has personal notes from board members on sticky notes attached will *always* result in a higher response.

2. How board members can help with the annual campaign:

> Most board members aren't enthusiastic about bringing a list of people from whom they will ask for money. Try some other, less threatening, ways to involve board members in fundraising.
>
>

- ◆ Make your annual gift first! Ask others to join you in supporting something meaningful and important.

- ◆ Provide testimonials for the fundraising letter. Be willing to endorse your organization, tell a personal story, and ask for support.

- ◆ Write personal appeal letters to names in your contact list.

- ◆ Use your social media sites to promote your organization.

- ◆ Make thank-you calls to donors. Participate in an annual thank-you event for major donors and supporters. Know who the major supporters are. Call to say thank you and write thank-you notes.

- ◆ Accompany staff on fundraising calls to donors and prospects.

- ◆ Host an event at your home or office. Invite friends and coworkers to learn more about your organization.

- ◆ Underwrite the cost of the mail campaign (printing, postage, etc.).

3. How board members can help with a major gifts campaign:

- ◆ Open doors for other board members and staff.

- ◆ Make a personal major gift and ask others to match it.

- ◆ Accompany staff on calls.

4. How board members can help with underwriting, sponsorships, and in-kind gifts:

- ◆ Research your own and other companies' giving programs.

- ◆ Write proposals and ask for sponsorships and underwriting.

- ◆ Solicit in-kind contributions of goods and services to reduce the expense budget, support fundraising events, and support programs and services.

5. **How board members can help with special events:**

◆ Plan it! Organize it! Serve on the committee! I don't know who wrote the book saying that this was the total responsibility of the staff.

◆ Sell tickets. Buy tickets.

◆ Solicit auction items and other things required to make the event a success. Solicit underwriting and sponsorships.

6. **How board members can help with planned giving:**

◆ Make a personal planned gift.

◆ Serve on the planned giving committee

◆ Solicit planned gifts.

7. **How board members can help with advocacy:**

◆ Contact lawmakers, testify, advocate! Individual contacts count for more than a single letter sent on behalf of the full board.

◆ Write letters to the editor to educate, clarify, and endorse your organization, being sure that the information is accurate and that permission has been granted by the board leader, for example.

Appendix C

Sample Board Member Job Description

Title: Member, [Organization] Board of Directors

Reports to: Board President (or Chair)

Role: Serve as a voting member of the board of directors for [the organization], developing policies, procedures, and regulations, and monitoring financial performance and [the organization's] programs.

Term: _____ years, beginning _____ and ending _____

Time expectations:

◆ Attend regularly scheduled board meetings, held on the _____ of every _____. The [organization name] bylaws state that board members must attend [state the requirement here].

◆ Participate actively in one or more committees of the board.

◆ Attend scheduled board retreats, planning meetings, workshops, or other board development activities.

◆ Attend, support, and participate in special organization events (you might list the important events and dates here).

Obligations:

- ◆ Fully understand and support the mission of [the organization].

- ◆ Establish policy.

- ◆ Hire, supervise, and evaluate the chief executive.

- ◆ Make an annual personal and/or professional financial contribution.

- ◆ Monitor the organization's financial performance.

- ◆ Develop and monitor short- and long-range planning and goals.

- ◆ Represent the organization to the public and private sector; serve as an advocate for the organization.

- ◆ Bring personal and professional expertise and that of others to support the organization's mission.

- ◆ Abide by the duties of care, loyalty, and honesty.

Appendix D

Sample Application for Board Membership

Thank you for your interest in serving as a member of the board of directors of [the organization]. Please complete the following questionnaire so that we can make the best use of your talents and expertise and offer you the most rewarding experience as a member of the board.

Name:_____

Business affiliation/title: _____

Mailing address:_____

_____

Business phone:_____ Home phone: _____

Mobile phone: _____ Email:_____

I will contribute these skills to the board:

❑ Accounting/financial

❑ Management

❑ Public relations

❑ Fundraising

❑ Investment

❑ Marketing

❑ Special events

❑ Community relations

❑ Lobbying

❑ Training

❑ Education

❑ Strategic planning

❑ Public speaking

❑ Other:_____

My experience as a member of other boards of directors includes _____

_____

_____

I will attend regular board meetings and special meetings .

❑ Yes   ❑ No

I can devote _____ hours per month to serve this organization.

I will attend a new member orientation.

❑ Yes   ❑ No

I will attend the annual board retreat.

❑ Yes   ❑ No

I will commit to an annual financial contribution of _____.

I want to become a member of this agency because_____

_____

Please provide references (use the back of this application).

Appendix E

Sample Conflict of Interest Statement

I agree to readily disclose any conflict or potential conflict of interest, making it a matter of record, either through an annual procedure or when the interest becomes a matter of board action.

I agree that I will not vote or use my personal influence on any matter that might constitute a conflict of interest. I will ensure the minutes of any meeting where this might occur duly show that I have abstained from voting due to the potential of or occurrence of a conflict of interest and that I have absented myself from the meeting during the voting process.

I understand that I may state my opinion or position on any matter described above, or answer pertinent questions to which I may lend my expertise, so long as I absent myself from a board vote on the matter.

I disclose the following conflicts of interest or potential conflicts of interest as defined in the current IRS Form 990 [quote the IRS Form 990 definition here]:

_____

Name

_____

Signature

_____

Date

Appendix F

Sample Board Member Annual Commitment Letter

I [_____] agree to serve as a member of the board of
directors of [_____]. I understand that my term of office begins
[_____] and extends for [_____] years, ending [_____].

As a member of the board of directors, I agree to:

❑ Abide by the bylaws and constitution of the organization

❑ Make an annual financial contribution of [_____]

❑ Attend all meetings of the board, including special meetings, unless excused

❑ Avoid any conflict of interest or appearance of a conflict

❑ Participate in short- and long-range planning activities

❑ Ensure effective fiscal controls and accountability

❑ Approve the annual budget

❑ Ensure [the agency] meets all legal and corporate requirements

❑ _____
   [Fill this in with any organization-specific commitment]

❑ _____
   [Fill this in with any organization-specific commitment]

❑ _____
   [Fill this in with any organization-specific commitment]

I agree that if I am unable to fulfill the commitments of a member of the board of directors of [the organization] at any time, I will give appropriate notice of resignation to the president (or chair) of the board.

_____

Name

_____

Signature

_____

Date

Appendix G

Parliamentary Procedures Simplified

Here are some easy rules of order that will help the board move business along in an orderly fashion. Whether or not you subscribe to the full *Robert's Rules of Order,* at least consider these simple rules so board members get in the habit of orderly business meetings. Demonstrate these procedures in your board meeting minutes and include them in your board policy and procedure manual:

- ◆ To introduce business, make a primary motion: "I move that . . ." You may not interrupt the speaker. The motion must be seconded. It is debatable and amendable and requires a majority vote to carry.

- ◆ To amend a motion: "I move that this motion be amended by . . ." You may not interrupt the speaker. The amended motion must be seconded. It is debatable and amendable and requires a majority vote to carry.

- ◆ To suspend further consideration about something: "I move we table [it]." You may interrupt the speaker. The motion must be seconded. It is not debatable or amendable. A majority vote is required to carry.

- ◆ To end the debate: "I move the previous question." You may not interrupt the speaker. The motion must be seconded. It is debatable and amendable and requires a two-thirds vote to carry.

- ◆ You may move to postpone an issue or decision until a further definite time by saying "I move we postpone this matter until . . ." The requirements are the same as those for ending the debate.

- ◆ To object to a procedure or personal affront: "Point of order." You may interrupt the speaker. No second is needed. The motion is not debatable or amendable and no vote is required. The chair decides the matter.

◆ To ask for a vote by actual count to verify a voice count: "I call for a division of the house." You may not interrupt the speaker. No second is needed. It is not debatable or amendable. No vote is required unless someone objects. In this case, a majority is required to carry the motion.

◆ To vote on a ruling by the chairperson: "I appeal the chairperson's ruling." It must be seconded. It is debatable but is not amendable. A majority in the negative is required to reverse the chair's decision.

◆ To adjourn the meeting: "I move that we adjourn." You may not interrupt the speaker. It must be seconded. It is not debatable or amendable. A majority vote is required to carry.

Index

If you enjoyed this book, you'll want to pick up the other books in the CharityChannel Press **In the Trenches™** series.

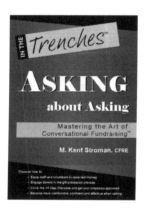

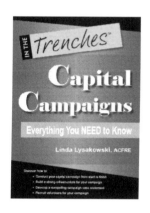

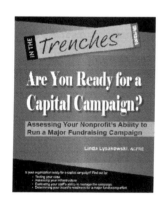

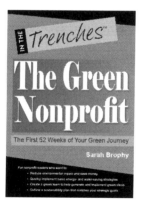

CharityChannel.com/bookstore

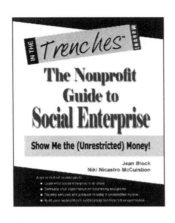

The Nonprofit Guide to Social Enterprise

Show Me the (Unrestricted) Money!

Jean Block
Niki Nicastro McCuistion

Getting Started in Prospect Research

What you need to know to find who you need to find

Meredith Hancks, MBA

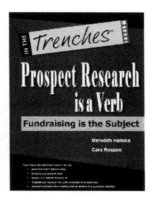

Prospect Research is a Verb

Fundraising is the Subject

Meredith Hancks
Cara Rosson

Goodbye Mission Statement; Hello Purpose

How to Harness Purpose as Your Most Powerful Management Tool

Cate Cardwell, BA

Opening the Door to Major Gifts

Mastering the Discovery Call

John Greenhoe, CFRE

Succeed in Your Nonprofit Funding Partnerships

Analyzing Their Costs and Benefits

Joanne Oppelt, MA, GPC

The Leaky Bucket

What's Wrong with Your Fundraising and How You Can Fix It

Ellen Bristol
Linda Lysakowski, ACFRE

Fundraising Research Made Easy

A Practical Guide for Fundraisers

Meredith Hancks, EdD
Cara Rosson

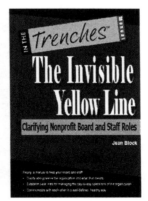

The Invisible Yellow Line

Clarifying Nonprofit Board and Staff Roles

Jean Block

CharityChannel.com/bookstore

CharityChannel
PRESS

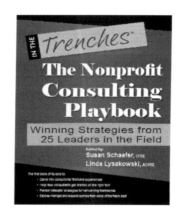

And now introducing **For the GENIUS® Press,** an imprint that produces books on just about any topic that people want to learn. You don't have to be a genius to read a **GENIUS** book, but you'll sure be smarter once you do!

ForTheGENIUS.com/bookstore

Made in the USA
Middletown, DE
13 June 2017